I Stood in the Flames

Snatching Victory From Disaster

Dr. Wanda Davis-Turner

Treasure House

An Imprint of
Destiny Image® **Publishers, Inc.**
P.O. Box 310
Shippensburg, PA 17257-0310

"For where your treasure is
there will your heart be also." Matthew 6:21

ISBN 1-56043-275-6

For Worldwide Distribution
Printed in the U.S.A.

Fourth Printing: 2000   Fifth Printing: 2002

This book and all other Destiny Image, Revival Press, MercyPlace, Fresh Bread, Destiny Image Fiction, and Treasure House books are available at Christian bookstores and distributors worldwide.

For a U.S. bookstore nearest you, call **1-800-722-6774**.
For more information on foreign distributors, call **1-717-532-3040**.
Or reach us on the Internet: **www.destinyimage.com**

Dedication

This book is dedicated to my parents, Bishop Lewis D. and Mary M. Stallworth, and to all those persons in my life, past and present, who were used by God to usher me into moments of victory when the cares and responsibilities of life set me up for many "fiery experiences." Satan intended for these experiences to destroy me, but God transformed them into platforms for victory and laughter.

Acknowledgments

Several months ago, a wonderful personal friend and sister in Christ urged me to "obey the leading of the Holy Spirit" and write books. Little did she know that she was confirming three prophecies that I was to write books for the Body of Christ. I want to take this opportunity to personally salute and thank her for her many days of encouragement, prayer, and support—Leona Weeks, you're the greatest!

A special thank you goes to the "love of my life," Andrew, who understood, sacrificed, and loved me throughout this entire process. Thanks also go to my beautiful daughters, Wendy, Whitney, Aneicka, and Andrea who, along with my sons-in-law Steven and Timothy, "suffered it to be so."

Special acknowledgments also go to Deborah Jones for her initial editing services and to Idella Sartin, my faithful administrative associate, who labored untiringly to see this project to its completion.

Contents

Chapter 1

Keep Your Feet
in the Face of Defeat

I was a young pastor's wife, the mother of two young daughters, and a busy Christian speaker, constantly speaking to women's groups around the United States and abroad. My husband, Bishop Wayne Davis, as the presiding prelate of World Won For Christ Ministries oversaw a thriving Christian fellowship of more than 348 churches and missions. His duties required him to continually teach, encourage, and financially assist churches around the world. After years of struggle and perseverance, we were "successful." We both had thriving ministries, and the future looked bright. Then Wayne flew to the Caribbean for a missionary trip.

I wasn't prepared for the phone call I received from Haiti a short time later. The voice on the other end said that Wayne was very ill, with serious breathing problems (later we learned that he had been struck by a deadly virus that had infected both of his lungs). Special arrangements had been made to fly him home for emergency medical treatment.

After I hung up, I suppressed the surging feelings of pain and panic and began to intercede for Wayne's life. It was during these hours of tearful intercession that the Lord showed me that my husband was too sick to make it all the way back to California. I would have to meet him when his flight from Haiti landed in Philadelphia, Pennsylvania—3,000 miles away from our home and church body.

I knew we didn't have the money for my airfare, so I told the Lord I would go to the East Coast, but He would have to supply the way. I needed a miracle, and there was only one Source. God miraculously provided me with a complimentary ticket from Los Angeles to Philadelphia, and within a few hours, I was standing at the gate waiting for Wayne to emerge from the flight. I couldn't believe what I saw...

The man I loved was now a mere shell and shadow of the healthy, vibrant man I'd kissed and sent off with a wave only two short weeks ago! Within 48 hours of our heartbreaking reunion at the airport, Wayne was not only hospitalized, but he was also rushed to the cardiac care unit of one of the nation's leading pulmonary hospitals.

When Wayne first arrived at the airport, he tried to act like everything was fine, despite his shocking appearance and weakened condition. At first he refused medical attention, saying that all he needed was a few days of rest. Despite my pleas that he go to the hospital, Wayne insisted that we check into a hotel in Philadelphia. We didn't realize it at the time, but God had also arranged for a leading pulmonary specialist to be staying on the penthouse floor of the same hotel.

Wayne suddenly fell seriously ill that night, and the front desk had the specialist immediately rush to our room! After he examined Wayne, this precious physician and I were finally able to persuade Wayne to check into the hospital.

Wayne hovered between life and death for ten days as teams of trained physicians and Christians alike battled for his life and prayed for a miraculous turnaround. Our church body in Inglewood, California, was in shock, and the international missions community was alarmed; but everyone was desperately praying for a miracle. They constantly battled thoughts of fear and despair, *What is happening to our leader?* As time went on, feelings of discouragement began to settle in: *Will he die? Is he really going to make it? Why is this happening to us?*

Meanwhile, I had my own battles to fight. One moment, I would sit quietly in the Intensive Care Unit trying to assess the crisis rationally and objectively. The next moment I would "report for duty" at the battlefront through uninhibited intercessory prayer, praise, and worship. If I had ever doubted the truth before, it now hit home like never before: If I wanted victory over this attempt on Wayne's life, then I would have to hook up with God and God alone! No one else could help me. No one else could give me the strength, courage, and hope I would need to win this battle for Wayne's life.

I soon realized that it was up to me, and the measure of faith God had given me to:

1. Maintain a local church budget of $100,000 per month, and
2. Keep up the morale of the administrative office staff as well as the ecclesiastical pulpit leadership to keep the "sheep from scattering."

You know the feelings I felt. I know you've felt the shock of unforgettable events or circumstances that hit you and seemed to usher you out of a perfect day into a night of crushing depression, fear, defeat, and deceit! What did you do when that time came? What did you do when your very soul and spirit cried out for encouragement, and everything within you looked to Heaven and cried, "Why?!"

Human beings are not designed to survive sustained periods of pain, depression, and sorrow. When these crises continue to assault us in unbroken waves, they can erode our souls like the breakers of a winter storm erode a shoreline. They can produce failure, defeat, and eventually, even death in our lives. That is why our Creator put something deep within our makeup that instinctively seeks solace in times of crisis. That place of the heart yearns for relief, help, aid, and refreshment. We are mere men and women who desperately need to be inspired and cheered up in the face of trouble and crisis. God never meant for us to go through the valley of the shadow of death and despair alone.

Although we habitually play games and hide from the truth when things are going well, once a crisis hits, we don't care where, what, or how God chooses to revitalize us—*we just want relief*! The situation may be bleak, devastating, or even suicidal; and every fact may militate against our survival. In the end, nothing matters as long as we can just find our Good Shepherd and sense His reassuring presence. In the dark hours of desperate need, our fancy public prayers and religious ways are quickly dropped in favor of a true prayer of the heart: "Lord, just find a way to encourage me and show me You care and I'll be all right!"

*Your attitude will
determine your destiny.*

Have you ever felt beaten, defeated, depleted, and just "out of it"? I'm talking about the time your attitude was so bad that you didn't even like yourself, let alone other people. You felt down, you looked down, and you talked down. I've learned the hard way that my attitude determines my altitude. This principle applies to everyone. Your personal attitude and posture determines how far you'll go in life. You can have a right attitude and land a job for which you don't even qualify, because your attitude will shape your destiny.

When you approach God for your needs, your attitude has a lot to do with what God can give you. If you don't really believe the promises in God's Word are for you, then your ability to receive answers to prayer will be permanently limited. If you dare to believe that all of God's promises are true for you, then you will receive everything God has for you!

If you dare to pray, "Whatever Your Word declares, God, I choose to believe that it is for me, and I want to receive it!" then you will get the overflow! Just ask God, "Lord, please dump Your blessings on me! Pour out Your blessings upon me." Elisha was bold enough (and "hungry enough") to ask God for a double portion of Elijah's anointing. You, too, must become obsessed about the things of God. Develop an extreme spiritual appetite for God's anointing and manifested power. You must also have an insatiable desire to receive God's blessings and experience His miracles. Your very attitude should be a sign that you are almost "greedy" about the things of God.

Public opinion will rob your dominion!

Satan knows your attitude determines your altitude. That is why he attacks your thoughts—he wants to enter your mind and plant doubts, fears, and lusts in your mind. It is through the thoughts of your mind that satan tries to affect and infect your attitude. If he can convince you to *think* that you are "down and out" or headed in that direction, then you will do and be exactly that! On the other hand, if you think *up* then you will *go up*! The Word declares, "For as [a man] thinketh in his heart, so is he" (Prov. 23:7a).

What do you think about yourself? Once you've been through the fire, public opinion should no longer matter. Don't worry about what your mamma said *wouldn't* happen for you. Don't worry about that mean uncle who "prophesied" that you would never amount to anything. Don't worry about the predictions of that school teacher who said you'd never grow up and would never graduate either! Learn to speak the Word of God to yourself. God has given you the power to render every "doomsday prophecy" spoken over your life *null and void*! However, it will never happen unless you get in the Word and see what God has said about you!

The day I received the bad news about Wayne's sudden illness, I turned to God's Word for the weapons of my warfare. I dug my favorite fighting sword out of the weapons' closet of Romans where God declared, "Nay, in *all these things* [tribulation, distress, persecution, famine, nakedness, peril, and the sword] we are *more than conquerors* through Him that loved us" (Rom. 8:37).

I didn't stop there! I kept building my armory until I *knew* I was going to win the battle. I strengthened my armor with the verses, "...he that toucheth you toucheth the apple of His eye. For, behold, I will shake Mine hand upon them, and they shall be a spoil..." (Zech. 2:8-9); and "The Lord will perfect that which concerneth me" (Ps. 138:8a). Just in case the enemy decided to attack from the rear with sin consciousness, I loaded my spirit with God's declaration, "...He hath made Him to be sin for us, who knew no sin; that we might be made the righteousness of God in Him" (2 Cor. 5:21).

I could have watched some soap operas and nursed my feelings of hurt and abandonment. I could have listened to the endless "helpful" comments of gloom and doom coming from other people, but I knew that if I did, I wouldn't have enough spirit or strength left to even get out of bed in the morning!

In those dark days when Wayne was lingering between life and death in Philadelphia, I knew that if I listened to people, I would never have the courage to stand behind another pulpit to preach or teach again! Out of desperate necessity, I learned to be *delivered* from public opinion! I had to settle the issue: it was *God* who called me to minister as a preacher, teacher, and counselor! *People* did not call me, *people* did not prepare me, and *people* did not send me, so I simply ignore the words of people and pay absolute attention to God.

I have to do this every day. I know what God has said about me in His Word, so I can no longer afford to concern myself with man's ever-changing opinions. That includes Mama's opinion, Aunt Lula Bell's opinion, and even the head deacon's opinion if they differ from the Word of God! Once you have heard from God, you must decide to choose His truth about you over the opinions of the public.

You must speak against the "doomsday prophecies."

Even when you know you have been called, confirmed, anointed, and affirmed by God, you will have those tired, exhausted moments when you wonder if you are going to make it. You can become grumpy and frustrated, *or* you can step aside for a moment of rest and pat yourself on the back in Jesus' name and arise again, rested, relaxed, and ready to go on a little further! If God has given you instructions to "do it," then trust God's wisdom and provision. You can do it exactly as God said you could: "For as [a man] thinketh in his heart, so is he" (Prov. 23:7a).

Your attitude is the expression of your "posture" in life. Your *posture* is your "mental position with regard to a fact or a state of being." Yes, I might be out of financial or personal resources, but that doesn't mean I'm broke or a failure! My "statistics" may look low, but my status is unlimited for "the earth is the Lord's, and the fulness thereof; the world, and they that dwell therein" (Ps. 24:1). I must always remember that God has declared, "For every beast of the forest is Mine, and the cattle upon a thousand hills" (Ps. 50:10). If God has all the cattle, and if I belong to God and am in covenant with Him, then His cattle are my cattle; for what God has, I have.

If "the earth is the Lord's," it then follows that the earth is mine also. It is perfectly natural for you and I to want to possess property with our name on the title deed. You can have it, because your Daddy has it. What my Daddy has is mine.

More than 20 years ago, Wayne and I had to file bankruptcy (I'll talk more about that later). One year later, God called us to open a new church in Inglewood, California. Now if I were God, I would not have called a man and woman to pastor who had such serious financial problems. However, God didn't ask for my opinion. God being God, He not only called us to pastor, but within the first year, He allowed us to *purchase* our first church property!

If that was not miraculous enough, the Lord also sent us a prophetic word that He was going to bless us with a new home! After a few moments of astonishment, we made a quality decision to agree with the word of the Lord. We immediately went "house shopping" and found a lovely Tudor-style brick home. We not only opened our escrow account with a "buy-with-faith-check," but we had the audacity to apply for a Veteran's Loan, knowing good and well that we had just filed bankruptcy less than 12 months earlier. After completing the loan application and fully disclosing our past financial problems, we were advised that our file would go to a special board for review and that we would be notified of their decision within 90 days.

We believed God and not the negative comments of our credit counselor, so we began packing in preparation for a move. Miraculously, in only five working days, we were notified that our Veteran's Loan application had been approved! The financial counselor was beside herself. She declared she had never seen anything like it!

---

*When you believe God,
He'll change the rules for you.*

What really happened? God promised in His Word that He would personally supply all our needs according to His riches—not according to our bank account or financial history (see Phil. 4:19). We needed a home, so we believed God, and God honored His Word by supplying the finances to purchase the home. When you believe God, He will change the rules for you. He will give you a job that you're not qualified for, and then He will see to it that you qualify for it each and every day, minute by minute, and hour by hour. God will literally teach you through people, places, and things, and show you just what you need to know to maintain and sustain His blessing in that position. All He wants to know is: "Can you believe? Can you get past defeat and discouragement and trust Me?"

Once you believe, God expects to see proof. He expects to see you act on your belief, for "faith without works is dead" (Jas. 2:20). If you really believe that God is your joy, strength, and preserver, then you won't let depression tie you to your bed to sleep away the day! If you really believe God, then no matter how depressed you feel, get yourself up and out of that bed and fix yourself up! Strip away those old dark, dreary, and drab colors. Replace them with bright red, vivid blue, and wonderful yellow. Get dressed and step out into God's earth and walk in God's joy. You will literally become stronger with every step you take!

You may be going through a storm in your marriage. Your spouse may have deserted you and the family. If you say that God told you that your mate was coming back home, then it is time to act as if God's Word is true! It is time to be wise. Begin *now* to prepare for your mate's return. Be a wiser spouse than you were when your partner left. Be willing to modify your lifestyle. Embrace the spirit of "change." Change the bad habits that your mate found irritating and frustrating. Change your diet, if necessary. Change your dress habits and get a new look that is attractive and appealing—*starting with your attitude*!

Change is always costly and uncomfortable, but it is necessary nevertheless. A new attitude will help you change in every other necessary space and place of your life. If you are a woman, and your spouse loves you with long hair (and your hair is short), then excite that mate! Go buy some hair! Glue it, weave it, or wig it, but do whatever it takes! If you have not been taking care of your mate sexually, then take some megavitamins and get before God. Ask Him to strengthen you so that you can "function at the junction." If you are really believing God to bring your mate home, then be willing to make sure that once your mate is home, he doesn't suffer lack!

Wisdom will change your attitude.

Too much of the time, most of the responsibility for "repairing a marriage" is put on the woman's shoulders, but God's message rings loud and clear to the man as well. In this day and age, women are starting to flee the nest too. Brother, if you were mean, cantankerous, stingy, and had an ugly, ungodly attitude before your wife left, don't expect to stay that way—even if God tells you your wife will return! You had better be prepared to change too!

Ask God to fix you up so that when she gets back, she has "something to come home to." If you were lazy and refused to work before she left, then screw your head on straight, fix your body up, and *go get a job*! Don't even bother to give God excuses; He is the one who bluntly declared, "If any [man] would not work, neither should he eat" (2 Thess. 3:10b).

Pull yourself together and change the atmosphere of your home by becoming a responsible husband your wife can be proud of! If the potbelly you've "developed" through years of neglect makes you look more pregnant than she ever was, then get your overflowing form down to the gym and work it off! (I'm sorry to be so blunt, but I might as well get it out quick so we can move on!) It might help if every time you do a push-up you say, "I'm pushing up for my honey. She's coming home."

Many of us want the Holy Spirit *to do what we're not willing to do.* Jesus sent the Holy Spirit to lead and guide us into all truth so that *we* could *do the work* of God's will ourselves.

> *When the Lord is your
> Shepherd, you shall not want.*

When you feel overwhelmed by the cares of life or feel despondent because of the demonic assaults that batter your spirit, you must bring your mind in line with the Word of God. Anchor your life upon what God says about you! Strengthen and stabilize your mental position with the Word of God.

Declare in your mind and speak with your mouth, "The Lord is my shepherd; I shall not want" (Ps. 23:1)! When you don't have another dollar in the bank account, when you don't know what to do next, just remind yourself over and over again, "The Lord is my shepherd; I *shall not want!*" Repeat the truth of God over and over again until the "facts" line up with the truth and your wants disappear! Your Source of supply is not dependent upon the economy. It is unchanged by your employer's decision to give or deny you a raise. Your Source isn't moved or depleted by your supervisor's opinion of you or your work (as long as you really do *work*). None of these has the power to alter God's promises or provision for your life!

When accountants and bill collectors call you on the phone, declare your mental position to be that of psalmist: "The Lord is my light and my salvation [and deliverance]; whom shall I fear?" (Ps. 27:1a)

Fearful and evasive parents raise fearful and evasive children. How many youngsters have been taught to fabricate lies by "Christian" parents who instruct their children to tell bill collectors, "Mommy is not home" while she quietly "steps outside" just long enough for junior to take the call? Isn't it time for us to just tell the truth? Tell the bill collectors, "I don't have the money right now, but I'm not running from you—I'm a godly person. I'm out of work, and I just don't have it. If you give me some time, I will get the money."

When God blesses you with the opportunity to get the money, don't lie—pay your debt. Don't spend God's provision on another pleasure while your debts go un-met and your word unfulfilled. And don't play the "religious game" either! Some Christians cry and beg for help to pay their rent or house note and then run off and spend the money designated for that purpose on new clothes or a trip to some Christian convention at an expensive resort! If God can't trust you to properly apply His provision to your obligations of honor, then He can't trust you with other blessings or greater provision!

When things get so rough and tight that the very fires of hades seem to be turned up on high, remember the warning in the Bible: "Yea, and all that will live godly in Christ Jesus shall suffer persecution" (2 Tim. 3:12). God says we are to persevere with patience and "count it all joy" (or act joyful) in spite of how we feel or what we see (Jas. 1:2).

"Are you saying that no matter what I'm going through, I'm supposed to act like I'm happy and full of joy?" Yes! Nobody should know what you're going through by your demeanor. People should be shocked when the Lord reveals your circumstances to them. Your outward appearance should never reflect what you are experiencing. Your appearance should reflect your state of mind, which is not based on circumstances but upon the unchanging promises found in the Word of God. Take your inner turmoil, fears, and uncertainties to the Lord in the privacy of your place of prayer. You will emerge with courage, guidance, and reassurance in God's promise and ability to provide!

You are not to walk around in denial, pretending that the fires of this life are not burning you up. But your outward expression should determine your genuine and unshaken belief in the Word of God! Many non-believers say Christianity is all "subjective" and not verifiable by empirical or outwardly visible data: It isn't "objective reality," and therefore isn't real or worthy of acceptance. This kind of belief is strong enough to hear every "fact" and face every "objective reality" without its foundation of truth being shaken! If I believe God's promise, "Beloved [that's you and me], I wish above all things that thou mayest prosper and be in health, even as thy soul prospereth" (3 Jn. 2), then I should immediately begin to think "prosperous thoughts." I should talk in prosperous terms and dress prosperously, and before I know it, I will *be* prosperous. Remember, as you *think* it, *speak* it, *walk* it, and *dress* it, you will *have it*!

---

*Your outward appearance
should never reflect your circumstances.*

Folks who look poor, talk poor, act poor, walk poor, and smell poor always tend to *stay poor*! If you are surprised that I said "smell poor," don't be. Poverty has a distinct smell. It stinks! When you purposely position yourself in poverty, most people don't want to come near you, much less help you! In fact, many times ruthless people will take what little the poor have and then turn their backs on them and their problems.

The fires of this life can escalate until you find yourself restless, impatient, upset, and uptight. What can you do if you are suddenly faced with a real financial crisis or fall into the fiery furnace of poverty? What can you do if an unexpected sickness threatens to strip you of your home, your marriage, and your financial security, leaving you alone with children, mortgages, ministry responsibilities, and more grief than you think you can bear? Like David, who found himself staring at the smoking embers of his burned-out hme and wondering how he would ever find his kidnapped family, *you have to encourage yourself in the Lord*—even when no one else will!

Chapter 2

Encourage Yourself

(Even If No One Else Will)

While Wayne was in the hospital battling for his life against the lung virus, my value of fax machines and telephone conference calls rapidly escalated. I was frantically juggling my roles as wife and Wayne's primary caregiver with my roles as a Christian leader and the mother of two daughters. And I was thousands of miles from home.

I had to quickly learn the responsibilities of an executive pastor. From the moment I received that phone call from Haiti, I became responsible for the pastoral care of the spiritual sheep God had put under our care. For the time being, I had to give instructions and encouragement to a congregation of more than 2,500 who were all more than 3,000 miles away.

At the same time, I was battling my own moments of isolation, loneliness, fear, and worry. No matter how many hats I wore, I still knew I was a human being who felt very inadequate to handle the pressures I was experiencing. One morning, at about 3:00 in my hotel room in Philadelphia, the enemy of my soul tried to slip in some paralyzing doubt and unbelief. In that desperate moment, the Lord stepped into the room and tapped me on the shoulder. The Holy Spirit told me, "Turn on your TV." When I turned on the television, the screen flickered, came into focus, and I saw Benny Hinn praying. He was asking Jesus to heal the sick and the lame! I bowed down on my knees before the Lord, and I heard the voice of Jesus whisper to me:

> *Be encouraged. As I use Benny Hinn, so shall I use you. Wipe your eyes, and fear not. I am with you. I won't leave you, nor forsake you. As soon as you can, get to one of Benny Hinn's crusades, and I will literally transfer his anointing to you.*

> *Don't worry about your husband, Wayne. I have a plan for his life. But know also that you, too, are important to Me; and I have plans for your life as well. I have grand and great plans! I know it does not seem like it now, but it is so.*

> *I love you, and I will care for you. You are My daughter. Stand to your feet! Praise and worship Me!*

With tears streaming down my face, I stood and worshiped the living God. A few minutes later, I dressed and left for the hospital, earlier than usual. The hospital was only blocks away, and when I walked into Wayne's room, he was connected to oxygen tanks and a room full of other medical apparatus. I laid hands on Wayne and prayed the prayer of faith. Within just four hours, he was removed from the Intensive Care Unit!

Two days later, Wayne was released from the hospital and sent back to recuperate at the hotel until the doctors could declare him strong enough to fly back to California without oxygen assistance.

Meanwhile, God was moving supernaturally on our behalf to perform miracles we knew nothing about. Every time I went down to the front desk of the hotel to ask about or pay our room charges, I discovered that *someone had beat me to the desk and anonymously paid the bill in full!*

A good friend of ours let us use his wife's car to commute between the hospital and the hotel, saving us another expense and inconvenience. Their wonderful son, a renowned chef in Philadelphia, personally prepared appetizing meals each day to encourage both of us to keep our strength up.

Meanwhile, God was also at work on the home front. A professional football player with the San Francisco 49'ers—at the extreme far end of the state—paid a $13,000 tax bill for us while I was away! A family from our local church collected all our bank notes and billing statements and paid all our bills from their own resources for one month—including our house payment, our car payments, all our utility bills, etc.! The list of God's provision through His loving people just went on and on.

One of God's miraculous blessings, though, I didn't discover until later. I once worked for an airline company as a customer service representative for just above minimum wage. The wages weren't anything to shout about, but the company offered a wonderful benefits package. I often asked God, "Lord, why do You have me working for this airline company as busy as I already am?" I never felt that God answered that question, but He did assure me that the day would come when I would understand His plan.

Eighteen months later, I resigned the position and the company offered me continued insurance coverage under its exceptional benefits package, and I maintained the policy by direct payment for several months.

One month before Wayne left for the missions trip to Trinidad and Haiti, I instructed our financial administrator to discontinue the medical insurance coverage under the airline's benefits plan. I distinctly remember saying, "No one in our family has been sick in a long time, and no one is presently ill. Perhaps this is an unnecessary monthly expense—cancel it."

Praise God for Spirit-filled and Spirit-led employees. Juanita sent in one more payment to the insurance company. Exactly 28 days later, Wayne became critically ill, and his hospital bill alone amounted to more than $90,000! Thanks to God's provision and intervention, our contribution to that medical bill was reduced to a mere $5.50!

In spite of the trouble, the crisis, and the heartache of that trial, God was perfecting everything that concerned me. He was blessing and encouraging me *in spite of me!* He wanted me to get to the place where I would learn to encourage myself in the Word! He wants all of us to learn that vital lesson of victory.

God wants you to be joyful
by faith and in obedience.

God's Word declares, "My brethren, count it all joy when ye fall into divers temptations" (Jas. 1:2). "Divers temptations" includes troubles, tests, sudden calamities, crises, and challenges. When you "count it all joy," you are saying you "reckon it" as a time to express joy. What this does *not* mean is that James wants you to walk around in denial. For instance, when the apostle Paul was beaten for preaching the gospel, I doubt that he was telling his torturers, "Oh, this feels great. Could you hit me a few more times, please?" No, I think Paul would tell you bluntly, "It hurt!" But he would also say, "In spite of the unspeakable pain, in spite of the terror of the moment, I count it joy to suffer for my Lord's name!" It was a joy for Paul to suffer, but it was *still* suffering (see Rom. 8:18).

Jesus is our perfect example, "...who *for the joy* that was set before Him *endured* the cross, *despising* the shame, and is set down at the right hand of the throne of God" (Heb. 12:2). The Word of God says the joy of the Lord is our strength (see Neh. 8:10). It was joy that gave Jesus Christ the strength to die for us. Joy will give you the strength to persevere in times of tests and trials too.

God wants you to be joyful by faith and in obedience, especially when you are in the fires of trial and trouble. It may not be a joyful circumstance, and it may not be an encounter that thrills you, but because your God is in charge of your life, you must act like it!

The three Hebrew youths, Shadrach, Meshach, and Abednego, didn't have much to rejoice about. Because they dared to trust in Jehovah God, they were about to be thrown in a fiery furnace. They did not realize that they were about to have the most exciting, life-changing, supernatural experience of their lifetimes, that right in the middle of their fiery trial they would come face to face with the Son of God! All they knew was that they could only serve the one living God—not a man proclaiming himself to be a god. They acted out their joy based on the things they *knew*, in spite of the things they could see. They succeeded, and the rest is history.

King Nebuchadnezzar looked into the furnace and was so astonished he scrambled to his feet. He saw the young men still standing in the flames! Then he said something that is as messianic and encouraging as nearly any other Scripture in the Bible:

> *He answered and said, Lo, I see four men loose, walking in the midst of the fire, and they have no hurt; and the form of the fourth is like the Son of God* (Daniel 3:25).

In the midst of sorrow, grief, and shock, you can act out joy because you are not in the flames alone! I know how you feel. During those times, you would probably prefer to have a spiritual tantrum—complete with the episode on the floor with all the kicking, yelling, and screaming! "I hate this! Lord, I'll have You know that I dislike this experience. It's not fair! Let me out of this furnace, God! Why me?"

This kind of dialogue can go on and on, but what if your eyes were opened so you could see the "other person" in the lonely room with you? What if, while you were lying on your back with your feet kicking in the air, you saw the pierced feet and hands of your Companion—the One who is patiently waiting for you to shut up so He can speak and comfort you?

God *never*, and I mean *never* sends you into a valley or fiery furnace alone! If you allow Him, the Holy Spirit will cause the Word of God to penetrate your thought processes and change your attitudes! His still, quiet voice will encourage you to choose the Word of God over your circumstances! He will turn your eyes away from your calamity and crisis to the Word and to the living Christ. Your troubles will shrink and dissolve in the face of your unbroken trust. Your attitude can change instantly with a simple decision, a decision of faith that promotes victory in the face of defeat, healing in the face of sickness, life in the face of death, and joy in the face of sorrow!

God's Word says, in effect, when you're going though the flames of tribulation, act like you're not. Put a smile on your face, pep in your step, and "reckon" yourself happy by faith! In your darkest hour of economic crisis, speak prosperity and look prosperous. Put on your best suit or select a brightly-colored "dress for success" outfit to reflect your faith, not your trial. Very often, when you look prosperous, then other prosperous people will flock around you, bringing both their wisdom and their wealth to bear in your life. Before you know it, you too will be on top financially—both encouraged and financially secure!

Poverty has a smell that will offend your ambitions.

On the other hand, if you focus on your problems instead of His promises and others think you don't have anything, they will try to take what you do have! When the fires of life are turned up and you get restless, impatient, upset, and uptight, you need to *encourage yourself*! Where or how do you encourage yourself? In and through the Word of God!

For as the rain cometh down, and the snow from heaven, and returneth not thither, but watereth the earth, and maketh it bring forth and bud, that it may give seed to the sower, and bread to the eater: so shall My word be that goeth forth out of My mouth... (Isaiah 55:10-11).

God's Word goes forth out of His mouth when it goes forth out of *your* mouth! You are the Body of Christ, God's mouthpiece to your generation. What have you been saying? What have you been speaking over your life, over your family's lives? What have you been speaking into your circumstances?

Jesus is the Head of the Church, and we are the Body. The word (God's Word) we speak shall not return unto us void (see Is. 55:11). In other words, you are going to get what you say, whether others like it or not. God will prepare a table in the midst of your enemies (see Ps. 23:5). He delights to bless you with prosperity—right in front of the people who despise the very ground upon which you walk!

Public opinion has nothing to do with the effect of God's Word in your life. God will bless you in spite of public opinion. They don't have to like you in the choir for you to get blessed. Deacons may resent you, but their opinions do not alter God's plan to bless you. God will bless you in spite of the fact that you are an "unappreciated" usher. The opinions of others have no power to influence, alter, or hinder the power of God's Word and His promise to supply all your needs!

When it is time for God's word to "go forth out of His mouth" to bless you, no one in Heaven or earth can stop it! According to Isaiah 55:11, His word shall accomplish what He pleases and shall prosper in the thing where He sent it! Encourage yourself with this powerful truth!

Even as I write these words, I must tell you that things are tight for me. However, I've learned what to do when I'm going through fiery trials. I turn to Psalm 27:14 and read, "Wait on the Lord: be of good courage, and He shall strengthen thine heart...." If you wait on the Lord and be of good courage, He will strengthen your heart. He'll strengthen your mind so you will be able to withstand the vain accusations of the devil when he whispers mocking words of failure and defeat in your ears.

A fact isn't always the truth. The real "act of encouragement" is the art of using truth to change facts. *Facts* are presented as having actual existence in your life, but this does not mean that facts are *truth*. Jesus Christ publicly stated that He is both the *Way* and the *Truth*—not a truth, or a source of truth, but He is *the Truth*. In other words, Jesus is the real thing. When you practice the art of using truth to change facts, you are really using Jesus (the Incarnate Word) to command the facts of your life to submit and conform to the power of truth.

John's Gospel says, "In the beginning was the Word, and the Word was with God, and the Word was God" (Jn. 1:1). John also said, "...the Word was made flesh, and dwelt among us..." (Jn. 1:14). This establishes that Jesus was the Word and that "all things were made by Him" (Jn. 1:3). These Scriptures prove that we have the right to take the Word, the Way, and the Truth, and put them against every life challenge!

(For the weapons of our warfare are not carnal, but mighty through God to the pulling down of strong

holds;) casting down imaginations, and every high thing that exalteth itself against the knowledge of God, and bringing into captivity every thought to the obedience of Christ (2 Corinthians 10:4-5).

We are authorized and anointed to command every thing that raises itself against the truth to bow down to the power and authority of the Lord Jesus Christ. It is exciting to know that the "facts" of our lives are subject to change at any moment. Facts are modified as new data is presented, but truth never changes, because Jesus is Truth, and His Word declares, "For I am the Lord, I change not" (Mal. 3:6a)!

You can change the facts with the truth.

Courage inspired by the Spirit confronts fear. When you inspire yourself or someone else with courage, that does not mean that you live a life without fear. It simply means that you are different because you will move against fear and do what you have to do, *in spite of the fear.* Courage is not the absence of fear; it is the act of confronting fear as you act out the Word you claim to believe.

When the "facts" of a threatening circumstance bring fear into your mind, those facts must be confronted by the *truth* of God's Word, which says, "For God hath not given us the spirit of fear; but of power, and of love, and of a sound mind" (2 Tim. 1:7).

It takes courage to put the veracity of God's Word above the reality of your circumstance! If your physician should tell you tomorrow that you have been diagnosed with cancer and that his diagnosis has been verified by the laboratory tests, those words could form an image in your mind. If they cripple you and steal the truth from your heart, those words could put you in the grave within 30 days.

If you want to be encouraged, then turn to the *truth* in the Word of God. Find out everything *God says* about healing—search for truth *in spite of the facts*! Yes, the doctor diagnosed you with cancer. It is a fact that the tests say "cancer." But is it the truth? The truth is what *God says* about you.

Come into agreement with God's words. Speak the words of God, believe the words of God, and act on the words of God in the Bible. Before you know it, you will be *living* out the truth of the Word. If you never hear or read His Word, you can't think or speak it, which also means you can't have it. Proverbs 7:1-2 says, "...keep My words, and lay up My commandments with thee. Keep My commandments, and live...."

Proverbs 6:2a says, "Thou art snared with the words of thy mouth." What you say is what you get. Start watching what you say, even in jest, because *words have power*. Since our enemy is not omnipresent, he relies on us to reveal our own weaknesses. Many of the things we say open up doors for satan to come in with his harrassment.

Encouragement revitalizes you.

According to the dictionary, encourage means, "to inspire with courage, spirit, or hope: hearten, 2: to spur on:

stimulate, 3: to give help or patronage to: foster."[1] When you're ready to give up, an encourager will get behind you and say, "Don't stop! You can make it!" How many times have you accomplished a goal because somebody got behind you and said you could do it? Even the most gifted among us get tired, discouraged, and tempted to quit at times. We all need to thank God for encouragers!

The truth will stimulate your mind and soul. You don't need to stimulate something unless it's lifeless or nonresponsive. Some of your dreams have died, and your personal visions are half dead. The spark has gone out of your life or marriage, and you need some stimulation to resurrect the dead! When a person's heart fails to receive life-sustaining oxygen, it goes into cardiac arrest and ceases to respond to the brain's urgent "wake-up call." Without stimulation and the restoration of blood flow, the vital tissues of the heart begin to die, and the death of the body will surely follow.

Hospital emergency teams will rush to the victim's bedside with all kinds of apparatus to *stimulate* the heart. Perhaps the most important piece of equipment is the defibrillator, which is used to apply an electrical shock to the heart. The hope is that this shock will stimulate the electrical mechanism of the heart to make it begin to beat again and regulate itself to pump blood with a normal sinus rhythm.

When somebody comes to encourage you, they are administering a dose of exhortation, encouragement, and hope. They are stimulating you, hoping you will kick

---

1. *Merriam Webster's Collegiate Dictionary*, 10th Ed. (Springfield, MA: Merriam-Webster, 1994).

back into the normal rhythms of life again. Sometimes in times of desperation they may just slap you with the truth. It may not always feel nice, but it will nearly always *stimulate* you into action, and it may cause you to fulfill your purpose.

*And David was greatly distressed...but David **encouraged himself** in the Lord his God* (1 Samuel 30:6).

David was in trouble, under stress, under pressure, and going through a storm. He was greatly distressed—*but...!* What you say after the word, *but*, can change your destiny! David was distressed and rightfully so. He was the son-in-law of Israel's king and the nation's most famous soldier. At one time he had associated with the most elite and powerful men of his day, but things had changed. He had been attacked by his own in-laws, and even by the king, his own father-in-law. His crisis landed him in a wilderness cave with the street thugs of his day, his only "army." Stripped of his privilege and right to sleep in the palace, he now slept with robbers and gangsters. He was actually leading a band of his former enemies!

Ironically, David was in the center of God's will. God knew those misfits and rebels would make good warriors in the hands of a great leader. (That is exactly why we shouldn't run from the people on the streets. Roughnecks, thugs, and prostitutes need to be saved too! Once they are converted and trained for the army of the Lord Jesus Christ, they are absolutely fearless in His service.)

Long before David became king, God put a fighter's spirit and mentality within him because he would need to fight a lot of battles on behalf of God's people. When

David had Saul's favor, the king "set him over the men of war" (1 Sam. 18:5). When Saul's heart turned, he ordered that same army to hunt down David and kill him. God led David to the "ghettos" of Israel and its surrounding nations to gather a people that most of us wouldn't want to meet in a dark alley. God gathered an army from the ghettos and anointed David to train and lead them so His divine purpose and destiny could be realized.

Even today, God is looking for people who are fighters, people who will go down before ever giving up! A lot of people will give up and lie down, but a fighter will say, "You're gonna have to take me out, because I ain't quittin'!" A fighter will fight you until his last breath. These are the kind of people God uses to lead His people into battle.

Jesus gave the keys of the Kingdom to Peter, the big-mouthed fighter. Peter had such a temper that he cut off a man's ear while surrounded by armed temple guards. He thought the man was going to harm Jesus so in a matter of seconds, he cut off the man's ear. Don't get upset about your personality. If you're a fighter, God can use you too. He will simply match you with others who will help you control your gifts. He may change your weapons and army assignments, but He wants you to keep that fighting skill.

Encourage yourself by recalling the victory testimonies of other believers. The Book of Revelation says they overcame "by the word of their testimony" (Rev. 12:11). Allow the testimonies of others to inspire you and build up your faith. Then you can begin building your own resumé of victories, blessings, and miracles!

But they that wait upon the Lord shall renew their strength; they shall mount up with wings as eagles; they shall run, and not be weary; and they shall walk, and not faint (Isaiah 40:31).

You have the power to fly high above the storm clouds of your problems and see beyond the momentary pressures with God's perspective. You will watch as God resolves them, and then swoop right back under the clouds and into the problem to be part of the solution, instead of part of the storm. God has not called you a little sparrow or a little robin; He says in His Word that you are like an *eagle*.

Although similar in size, build, and strength, eagles and buzzards are very different. The biggest difference between an eagle and a buzzard is their *diet*. Eagles are predators that primarily catch live fish and small and medium-sized prey. Buzzards eat dead things. They thrive on carrion, the carcasses and remains of things that have died off. If you eat the lies of satan, you are a spiritual "buzzard." Satan wants you to feed on dead images that are in a state of putrefaction. He wants you to feed on the rotten things he brings into your life. Eagles eat living food. What is the liveliest food you can eat? The Word of God. Eat the words of Jesus and you can be a eagle.

When you eat the right food, you can fly like an eagle.

Your faith in the Word of God will bring endurance to run in the strength of God instead of your own weakness.

He will remove your weariness through His strength, and put you back in the race. It is when you see victory just around the corner that the enemy tries the hardest to push you down or trip you into defeat. In fact, the enemy will send the entire "Press family" against you—Brother Depress, Sister Oppress, and Cousin Suppress! Just keep your focus on the joy set before you, the good pleasure of your King! Don't even recognize the existence of the "Press family." Don't speak to them, and don't receive *a single thing* from them.

I heard a man of God tell a story about a man who was dying of starvation. Doctors came to the man's bedside and said, "Sir, you have ten minutes to live. All you have to do is eat this soup and bread and drink this water and you can live! Do you believe that?" The man whispered, "Yes, I believe it." Five minutes later the soup, the bread, and the water were still there.

Again, the doctors came to the man's bedside and pleaded, "Sir, you have only five minutes to live. All you have to do is eat this soup and bread and drink this water and you can live. Do you believe that?" The man answered, weaker than before, "I believe it."

At the end of the tenth minute, the man dropped over dead while the food still sat on the table untouched. Why did the man die? He *believed* the food could save him, but *he didn't act upon what he believed!*

David was so overwhelmed by his circumstances and frustrated by his inability to change them, he said (echoing the pain and suffering endured by the Messiah hundreds of years later):

I am poured out like water, and all my bones are out of joint: my heart is like wax; it is melted in the midst of my bowels. My strength is dried up like a potsherd; and my tongue cleaveth to my jaws; and Thou hast brought me into the dust of death (Psalm 22:14-15).

David was pressed beyond his ability to endure. This man who was known as God's worshiper, God's warrior, and God's anointed king, began to doubt, fear, and give up his blessings! David was human. Every part of his body and spirit was so attacked by circumstances that the great psalmist became *discouraged.* What can turn around our discouraged spirits, minds, and hearts when the powers of satan press us this hard? How did David arise from the cave of despair to the palace of a king? David declared, "I will encourage myself! I will cry out to the Lord!"

"But be not Thou far from me, O Lord: O my strength, haste Thee to help me" (Ps. 22:19). David was saying, "God, I may be broke, I may be sick, and I may be tired and burned-out in spirit, soul, and body; but Lord, in the midst of my burnout, *I see You!*" You must get to the place where you become desperate to see God—even in the midst of your own burnout.

What did David say during his low point in life? He screamed out, "Unto Thee, O Lord, do I lift up my soul. O my God, I trust in Thee: let me not be ashamed, let not mine enemies triumph over me" (Ps. 25:1-2). David lived in the real world. He desperately needed the Lord to "lift his soul" because he had been dropped in the throes of depression, sorrow, and discouragement—just as we are today!

David did not blame God for his discouragement or for the circumstances creating his sorrow and depression. He didn't "command" the Lord to rescue him before he would begin dialogue and communication with God either. Many of us get so angry and misguided in our judgment during times of discouragement that we shake our fist at God and demand, "If You want me to pray, or worship, or sing praises to You again, then lift me out of this trouble first!" David realized that he must take responsibility for his own state of mind. God had not dropped him, so he did not waste time blaming God. He took the responsibility himself to pray, "Unto Thee, O Lord, do I lift up my soul." Too often we want *God* to lift our soul, but God has already *equipped us* through His Word to lift up our own soul!

At some point, we must decide to agree with God's Word and trust Him to bless us rather than curse us. Too many of us have become *quitters*. We need to wipe that word from our vocabulary. Don't be stopped by your age, your finances, or by public opinion! If you have a goal to increase your education, then enroll in school and don't stop until you graduate with honors! Discipline your mind and accomplish each and every vision God has given you. Stop looking for "shortcuts" and get back on the road to success.

Truth doesn't change.

Make sure the opinion of God and His Word count more to you than public opinion. His Word will lift you from guilt to grace. It is His Word that declares emphatically, "He which hath begun a good work in you will perform it until the day of Jesus Christ" (Phil. 1:6b).

Do you want to encourage yourself? Get up from your depression and sorrow. Turn from your own guilt or grief and *encourage someone else!* Give someone else the truth and alter the "facts" of their life. Introduce them to the God of truth, who can change facts at any given moment. God can just think about you and instantly snatch you out of poverty. He can simply *think* about your family and relocate you to "Prosperity Avenue." With a thought, God can impact your body and restore your health. Facts are subject to change, but truth doesn't change. Jesus, the Incarnate Truth, is "...the same yesterday, and to day, and for ever" (Heb. 13:8). "God is not a man, that He should lie" (Num. 23:19a).

I found a wonderful, exciting poem written by Benjamin Antrobus of London in the year 1715:

Concerning Sufferings

Surely those People who through Faith
In Christ, on God depend
Need not to fear the Rage of Man,
The Lord will them defend.
Though wicked men rise up, and come
God's people to annoy
Yet they shall disappointed be,
His saints they shan't destroy:
Therefore ye need not for to fear,
When you assembled be;
Nor yet ought you to make escape,
And from them for to flee;
Because, except the Lord doth grant,
And give to Satan leave,
He has no Power to do you harm:

This Doctrine pray receive;
That in the Faith you firm may stand,
And patiently may bear
Those sufferings that may attend,
Casting on God your Care;
Who careful is, them to support
That witness to his Cause,
And never fails to give Relief
To those that keep his Laws.

It is amazing that this poem, written hundreds of years ago, still rings true today. It serves as yet another witness and exhortation for you to encourage yourself!

Chapter 3

God's First Miracle!

"Hey God...are You listening? I have traveled all over this country teaching and preaching that You are a healer. I know that I know that I know that by Your stripes, we are healed (see 1 Pet. 2:24). I even testify with a grateful heart of Your miraculous healing power in my own life when You healed me of cervical cancer. Now, God, I'm still waiting on You to heal my husband, Wayne. Now look, Lord...I'm tired of traveling to meetings, conferences, and revivals without being able to open my sermon with a confirmed report that Wayne is healed and back in his pulpit preaching. I tell You what, if You don't hurry up and give me my miracle, I'm going to stop preaching and teaching until You do! Is that clear, Lord? I need a miracle and I need it now. And this is the miracle that I need: *Heal Wayne and do it now!*"

*This **beginning of miracles** did Jesus in Cana of Galilee, and manifested forth His glory; and His disciples believed on Him* (John 2:11).

Miracles are recorded throughout the Scriptures. Not a day goes by without saved and unsaved people from every tribe, tongue, and culture saying, "I need a miracle!" Even though most human beings want a miracle to fulfill a desired end or bring relief from a crisis, the true purpose of miracles extends far beyond one person's need.

Miracles consist of more than "God giving you what you think you need." According to John's Gospel, Jesus "began to perform miracles" to *manifest His glory* and *generate belief* in Himself.

The Greek term translated as "manifest forth" is *phaneroo*. It means "to make visible or known what has been hidden or unknown, to make visible, and realized; to expose to view, to show one's self, to be plainly recognized."[1]

God moves if it will fulfill His purpose.

Jesus was manifesting His *glory*, which comes from the Greek word, *doxa*. It means "to honor, praise, worship: majesty; a thing belonging to God: the kingly majesty which belongs to Him as supreme ruler, majesty in the sense of the absolute perfection of the deity; a thing belonging to Christ: the kingly majesty of the Messiah, the absolutely perfect inward or personal excellency of Christ."[2]

The same verse tells us that when Christ Jesus manifested His glory, the disciples *believed* on Him. The Greek

---

1. James Strong, *Strong's Exhaustive Concordance of the Bible*, ((Peabody, MA: Hendrickson Publishers, n.d.), #5319. (These meanings also come from their prime root words, and so definitions may not precisely match *Strong's*.
2. *Strong's Exhaustive Concordance of the Bible*, #1391.

word for *believe* is *pisteuo*. It means "to believe, commit unto, to commit to (one's) trust, to think to be true; to be persuaded of; to place confidence in."[3]

Miracles occur to reveal Jesus and His kingly majesty. Miracles always bring Jesus honor, praise, and worship. You don't acquire a miracle just because you need or want one; you receive a miracle when the satisfaction of your need in is line with God's plan to bring praise and honor to Jesus Christ.

God doesn't perform miracles just because we say He should or because we decree that He will. He moves if it will fulfill His purposes. Jesus will work miracles to bring glory and praise to the Father and to ignite the passionate fire of worship among His people. The Word of God says:

> *Now unto Him that is **able to do** exceeding abundantly above all that we ask or think, according to the power that worketh in us, **unto Him be glory in the church by Christ Jesus** throughout all ages, world without end. Amen* (Ephesians 3:20-21).

Your motive for seeking miracles cannot be self-centered, or there will be no miracles—no matter how long you fast and pray! You may be upset with God for this very reason. If you asked Him to supersede your lousy credit and miraculously bless you with a car in answer to your demand, then you were probably disappointed. Listen: It doesn't take a miracle to buy a car! Just pay your bills, keep your credit up, and save your down payment. God will only override your bad credit and correct it if He is

---

3. *Strong's Exhaustive Concordance of the Bible*, #4100.

going to get the glory out of His intervention. He doesn't work miracles of that magnitude so a poor steward and undisciplined spender wearing a Christian name tag can strut around bragging about his new car to everyone, "Look what I have!"

God is probably waiting to see if you will bring some people to church in that car! He's looking to see if you will pick up a homeless person and buy him something to eat to show him the practical side of God's love before you introduce him to Jesus. Now that would give glory to Him!

You must need a miracle before you can receive one.

God will not grant you anything that is not rightfully yours! Miracles motivate and incite people to trust Jesus and commit their lives to His purposes. Miracles manifest when someone requests a supernatural intervention of God that will bring honor and glory to the Lord Jesus! Your need for a miracle must add to the cause of Christ.

God is under no obligation to honor your request when your want, desire, or need does not honor or glorify Jesus. For example, a desire to take a married woman's husband as your own husband does not honor or glorify Jesus—it dishonors His Word and His principles for holy living. God will not give you anything that is not rightfully yours. If you scheme, cheat, or deceitfully receive a gift, then do not praise God for the gift; it is not from the Lord. You have stolen the gift, and you have given satan, the thief, permission to enter your life to destroy you and extract the most precious and holy thing in your life, your relationship with God.

Miracles are not given solely for our direct benefit. They occur to manifest the glory of God and to inspire faith and belief in human hearts. We are called to glorify God and position our hearts to be in the state of believing, trusting, and knowing Jesus. That is called *faith*. A survey of the New Testament shows that if your healing, if your resurrection from the dead, if your deliverance, or if your prosperity brings glory, honor, praise, and commitment to Jesus, then *look out!* You are in line for a miracle!

Miracles happen based upon their significance to the cause of Christ. That is why Jesus could walk up to the pool of Bethesda and heal just *one man* out of several hundred equally desperate people clamoring for healing (see Jn. 5:2-19). He healed the one man and then walked away without another word. Although Jesus had the power and authority to heal every person on the planet that day, He only healed the one man described in Scripture, because He *only* did those things His Father instructed Him to do (see Jn. 8:28).

Every benefit we experience in life must be the result of our obedience to our heavenly Father. That afternoon at the pool by the sheep gate, the Father instructed the Great Shepherd to heal "one man." Jesus obeyed and the man was healed before hundreds of witnesses. The miracle brought honor and glory to God, and exposed the hypocrisy of the religious leaders who were more interested in the letter of the Law than in the miracle-working power of God. For centuries, that miracle has inspired countless songs, sermons, and Sunday school teachers all over the world who have ignited the spiritual appetites of youngsters with the exciting details of the man at the pool called Bethesda.

If you need a miracle—if you need to see God supernaturally intervene in the affairs of your life—then it is absolutely paramount that you *get God's attention!* One of the best ways to get the attention of God is to call upon the Lord in praise and worship, despite your circumstances, challenges, or troubles. Give God what He adores and desires: your praise and worship.

Praise gets God's attention.

You were created to praise God. When you learn to praise and worship Him, you are exercising your highest level of giving—and when you give, you receive. When I am in pain, or sickness is trying to destroy my body (even when my diagnosis is devastating and the prognosis deadly), I begin to worship and praise God for being *Jehovah-Rapha*, God my Healer. I extol His wonderful and great name and boast of all His great works! I praise God with my mouth, my hands, and my feet. I lift up His name beyond my pain, beyond every curse of cancer, diabetes, ulcers, tumors, heart disorders, and so-called terminal diseases— even beyond irritating nuisances of bunions, corns, and other skin irritations.

I overcome my circumstances and soar beyond the limits of "empirical logic" and I defy my intellect in favor of God's unlimited wisdom and power. What happens in exchange? God responds to my praise and worship by supernaturally intervening in the affairs of my life to produce a great and wonderful *miracle*!

If you discover the true power of praise and worship, you will automatically turn to God every time a dilemma enters your life. Unfortunately, most of us complain instead. We spend our time calling *other people*, hoping they can rescue us out of our dilemma. All too often, we expect others (i.e., bankers, parents, landlords, employers, friends, and relatives) to supply all our needs. Then we get mad when they don't want to loan us their money after we have wasted ours!

It is not the responsibility of our friends, relatives, employees, employers, pastors, or parents to meet our needs—especially when God is waiting for us to get His attention. He dwells in the midst of praise. He loves it when you give Him attention while driving down the street. All the drivers alongside you may look at you like you have lost your mind as you raise your hands in excitement and shout, "Jesus, I love You! Jesus, I praise You!"

He loves to see you shut down the vacuum cleaner and put down the cleaning cloths just to give Him your full attention as you say, "God, I thank You!" He loves it when you suddenly speak to Him while typing letters at the office, "God, You've been so good to me! Thank You!" He loves your adoration and praise. You have to get to know your God. You must worship Him!

Learn to touch God! God loves for you to "rub up against Him and *touch Him*" through your praise and worship, as you talk to Him. Jairus, the ruler in the New Testament who asked Jesus to heal his daughter, won the attention of Jesus by *bowing down in worship*. This was a great ruler and senior elder of the Temple, yet with all his spiritual, legal, and social authority, he actually bowed down in the dirt before Jesus in a crowded public place to openly acknowledge the authority of Christ the Savior, the Healer. He was serious about getting a miracle!

What about you? Do you exercise authority over your life? Do you rule over your financial affairs? How about the words of your mouth? Does God have trouble getting you to drop your pride long enough to acknowledge Him as King, Lord, and the Redeemer of your life? You would rather suffer than bow in worship. You would rather remain impoverished than bow to the Lord! You would rather see your marriage end in a divorce court than humble yourself before the Lord in worship and praise!

Touching Jesus with worship is the most powerful act of faith you can make.

Jairus had *real authority*, yet he knew that to get his miracle, he first had to get the attention of the Miracle-Giver! He chose the highest level of regard he could offer his Lord and Savior—he offered the Lord worship. The woman with the issue of blood *touched* Jesus in another powerful form of worship. True worship in "spirit and truth" will touch Jesus (see Jn. 4:24). Touching Him is the most powerful act of faith you can make, because your touch demands a response from Jesus. It communicates the message, "Lord Jesus, out of everyone in my life, You are the most important." Jesus has given more for you than anyone else in the universe, and He deserves to be the most important person in your life.

Worship precedes the release of miracles in the lives of people throughout the Bible. The leper who followed Jesus on the road won Jesus' attention through his uninhibited worship. David went from a forgotten shepherd boy to Israel's greatest king because at a young age he learned how to praise and worship the true and living God of Israel.

To worship God is to acknowledge Him for who He is. The friends of the paralytic man acknowledged Jesus as the Healer when they brought their friend to Jesus for healing. Their faith made a way where there was no way when they boldly broke through the roof of a crowded house to reach the Master within. Jesus not only healed the sick man and told him to walk, but He also forgave the man's sins! All this came about because the man's friends had the wisdom to acknowledge God and His power.

If you ever get so sick that you can't pray for yourself, then you had better be hanging around with the right people! Don't associate with somebody who doesn't believe in God or His ability to work miracles. Otherwise, you will fall when trouble hits your life! I run with deeply spiritual people. No, I'm not talking about folks that *look* deep and *talk* deep; I'm talking about people who are *deep into prayer, deep in their praise, deep in their shouting, deep in their singing,* and *deep in God's Word*! If you scratch them, God comes out!

If the time comes when I am too burdened, sick, or weary to pray for myself, I can hear their fervent voices in my spirit, praying for me without ceasing! That paralyzed man lying on the pallet received his healing because he had friends who worshiped Jesus. A dear intercessor in my church told me on one occasion that she asked God, "What is my pastor going through?" She said a headache hit her so severely that it literally knocked her to the floor! She could barely call for help. When she finally came to herself, she begged her little five-year-old daughter, "Just put your hands on me and pray for Mommy. Go get Daddy, and call the saints!" The pain was that bad. She said God told her that there were times that her pastor's pain was so bad that he couldn't pray. God told her, "Quit asking him to pray, and quit asking him to quote Scripture. Be a friend to him. Quote those Scriptures for him, and pray that prayer *for* him!" There are times when friends need to be true friends in times of adversity and *believe God for the miraculous*!

Jesus healed the two blind men who acknowledged Him and performed the other miracles reported in the New Testament because they benefited the cause of Christ. Those who needed a miracle won His attention through praise and worship. Praise celebrates Jesus, and worship acknowledges Him for who He is. We celebrate people by saying good things about them and what they have accomplished.

The first step to a miracle is to send for Jesus. The Lord's *first miracle* happened because somebody invited Jesus to a wedding! Who are you inviting to "your happening"? The Bible says when you acknowledge Him in all your ways, He will direct your path (see Prov. 3:6). Whatever comes, wherever you are, and whenever trouble hits you, make sure you invite Jesus there too. Don't go where Jesus isn't; it's too dangerous! Don't get in your car and drive to work if Jesus is not in that car.

Don't go into the supermarket thinking you're going to walk in safety without Jesus at your side. Don't even walk to your mailbox to pick up your mail without Jesus. You need Him every hour, and every moment of your life.

Obedience engages your miracle. Surround yourself with people who believe in your Jesus. Mary, the mother of Jesus, gave some people the most important advice of their lives. She said, "Whatsoever Jesus says unto you, do it" (see Jn. 2:5). The thing that locks your miracle in is *obedience*, not understanding. God is working for us behind the scene, underneath the scene, and on top of the scene! He is doing great things for us, and all God wants from us is our praise, our worship, and our obedience. When you need a miracle, do not waste time trying to "logically understand" God's instructions, just obey the commands of the Lord instantly and see the miraculous results.

Obedience will set you up for your miracle.

If you want a miracle, learn to move when God says "move"! Don't do what you want to do if you're looking for a miracle. You cannot socialize and fraternize with whomever you wish. Learn to wait God's way. The Israelites had to follow the cloud. When it moved, they moved; when it stood still, they stayed in the camp. The Church needs to learn this lesson in our day. We need to go when and where the Spirit leads, not where it feels most convenient or comfortable!

Obedience opens the door for Jesus to set you up for a miracle. You can't obey if you don't believe. When you believe, you will obey, and when you obey, you will receive. Look closely at the Lord's first public miracle:

> *And there were set there six waterpots of stone, after the manner of the purifying of the Jews, containing two or three firkins apiece. Jesus saith unto them, Fill the waterpots with water. And they filled them up to the brim. And He saith unto them, Draw out now, and bear unto the governor of the feast. And they bare it. When the ruler of the feast had tasted the water that was made wine...*[he] *saith unto* [the bridegroom]...*thou hast kept the good wine until now* (John 2:6-10).

For some reason, Mary came to Jesus when she learned her hosts were out of wine for the wedding feast (see Jn. 2:3). We don't know if she expected Him to buy it or work a miracle, but we do know she expected Jesus to fix the problem, and both of them knew it would reveal His true identity and bring glory to God. It was then that Mary instructed the servants in the house to obey Jesus, and the six waterpots are first mentioned. The Scripture states that the waterpots were "set." In other words, they were appointed to be right where they were on the floor at the wedding. They were a vital part of God's setup for the Messiah's first public miracle at the wedding feast. They were, in fact, put there by design to hold, or "house" the much-needed miracle. They were not vessels of ornament, and they weren't just fixtures. They were vital instruments of God's purpose set in place to bring a miracle (and publicly reveal the greatest of all miracle workers) to His people.

Miracles defy logic, but they express the wisdom of God. Many things in your life may seem to be unnecessary.

They may appear to lack beauty and be out of place, at best, yet God does not want you to throw them away! Why? They're not useless, nor are they unnecessary. Like the large waterpots in Cana, those things have been set in your life for God's purpose: They may be holding your miracle! They might be ugly, broken, fire-blackened, or "in the way," but they have been set there.

You may be ready to throw away that "black pot" that other people would call your spouse, while God has planned to deliver your greatest miracle through that "pot." You may be planning to get away from that stubborn, cantankerous pot, but God says, "Wait a minute! That 'pot' may be useless to you, but it's *your* pot. It has been sovereignly set there to give you your miracle!"

You may be ready to walk away from the place of employment that *God has ordained* to hold your miracle. "You don't understand, Lord. Someone has offered me a better title with more money!" You had better make sure God isn't saying, "You are about to leave the place I've designed for your miracle!" If God set you there, then He wants you to stay right there until He moves you again. It may seem uncomfortable, and certainly inconvenient, but don't leave the party until it's over. When God is invited to a party, the best things often happen at the last. Don't abandon the pot that may contain your miracle!

"Jesus saith unto them, Fill the waterpots with water. And they filled them up to the brim" (Jn. 2:7). Have you ever been in a financial pinch when God came along and spoke to your heart, "Find $20 somewhere and go open up a bank account"? If you have, then you probably said something like, "God, I don't have a job, and I don't have money coming in at all. In fact, I will have to borrow this

$20 to even obey Your word to me. Now why would You have me borrow $20 to open up an account?"

God knows what you don't know, and He knows what He can't afford to tell you (for your own good): The checking account you open will become your waterpot. There's a miracle in the making with your name on it. In fact, your miracle was declared even before you were placed in your mother's womb! God just wants to get you to a place of immediate obedience. Too often, we offer God "selective obedience." However, you must give God *immediate obedience* if you want a miracle! The Word declares, "To every thing there is a season, and a time..." (Eccles. 3:1). When your waterpot is empty and you are in a state of immediate obedience, God will bring your miracle to you in spite of the bleakest circumstances.

Miracles need your input.

I was raised in a Pentecostal family, and my dad, Bishop Lewis Stallworth, was a great preacher of faith. He resigned his well-paying government job when God led him to become a full-time pastor in the small agriculture town of Stockton, California. It seemed like the power of God was manifested in my family's life on a daily basis! In fact, it was a genuine miracle of faith that our family of 13 children ate, slept, and were clothed each day!

Many times, Dad's stipend at the church included tithes of fruit and vegetables, especially during spring and summer months, since most of the families in the church harvested fruit, vegetables, and cotton. In the midst of sometimes dire circumstances, God gave Dad a command to build a "real temple." It was to be made of brick, despite our lack of funds. The church, and our family in particular, became the laughingstock of Stockton, as we operated by faith and dug a hole in the ground for the "temple basement." People would drive by and say, "Bishop, why don't you just fill it with cement and call it a large swimming pool!"

My father, the Bishop, replied by selling our family home and property by faith to help purchase the land for the new temple. After we moved into a parish residence, the Stallworth family began to see the supernatural moving of God as God performed one miracle after another! An architect designed the building, and engineers soon became involved in the project. Then a family construction firm took over the vision and saw it to its completion! Today, that "temple" still stands as a monument to the power of the Living God and the faith of His people.

It was during this long process of faith that I began to see how God constructs miracles. Above all, I learned that miracles don't just happen—they are created. Many a day, I went out with my brothers and sisters to sell block tickets to help purchase the beautiful brick and floor tiles for the wonderful temple in my father's vision. In the winter, we made delicious peanut brittle by the barrel to help to furnish the temple with beautiful pews and church furnishings. I knew God would perform the miracle, but I also noticed the He always invited *our participation* too! Throughout the years, this principle of co-laboring for miracles has been relived again and again.

Later in my life, I encountered complications during the third month of my first pregnancy, just as I was entering the second trimester. I was ordered to stay in bed for over three months, and I experienced a continuous season of depression and anxiety that resulted in an eating binge. I began the pregnancy at 113 pounds, and at delivery, I weighed over 180 pounds. I thought I would be "rewarded" with a Caesarean section delivery, but my doctor advised that I deliver the baby by natural vaginal birth to straighten out a tilted uterus.

When the time came, I was in labor for 48 hours in the hospital, and still there was no baby. I was about to lose my mind because I had internalized the pain and stress. My husband and mother pleaded with the doctors to do something, but to no avail. I remember turning my face to the wall and silently telling Jesus, "I can't take anymore. Please, help me!"

The next minute, the door to the labor room opened and Rev. Joseph Garlington of Pittsburgh, Pennsylvania, walked in! This dear family friend was visiting our church as a guest evangelist at the time, and he came to pray for me. He quietly and gently held my hand as he asked the Lord to send an angel to bring me speedy deliverance, and then he slipped out of the room.

Within four or five minutes, a beautiful Asian nurse entered my room and wiped my forehead as she gently said, "You're still here! We will have to do something about this. Be still, and let me examine you." By that time, I had been in labor so long that I was almost out of my mind. My spirit was broken, and I couldn't cry, scream, or yell. I just lay there, trying to pretend none of this was happening to me.

The nurse apologized in advance for causing more pain, and then she said, "I need to puncture your water bag and get this baby delivered." Within ten minutes, my beautiful 9-pound 7-ounce baby girl entered the world.

The next day, my husband and I wanted to express our appreciation to the wonderful nurse who came to my aid in my eleventh hour, but when we asked the doctor who she was, he looked at us strangely and said, "We have no Asian nurse in this unit." I told him he had to be mistaken, and described her in detail. Again he said, "I'm sorry, but we have no Asian nurse." The Holy Spirit reminded me in that moment of Rev. Garlington's prayer, and I knew the truth—*God had sent an angel!*

Many times, the miracle vessels God places in your life are heavy. The waterpots in Cana were very heavy, even when they were empty. Can you imagine how heavy they were once they were filled with water? The servants of the house sealed their master's miracle when they obeyed the Lord's commands (without protest or complaint). They not only obeyed by filling the pots with water, but the Bible says they filled them "to the brim."

Don't see how little you can get away with. When God asks you to do something, *go all the way.* Take it to the brim and beyond no matter how hard or heavy the task seems. *There's a miracle waiting on the other side of obedience!*

Miracles laugh in the face of doubt! Water symbolizes life, and in the Bible blood is considered the substance of life. Even after the waterpots in Cana were filled to capacity with water, the servants saw no miracle because another step of faith was required. Jesus told them to take some of the water from the pots to the governor of the feast. The servants probably thought, *This is crazy! First we filled up these pots with water like He asked, and now He wants us to take some of this water to the governor of the feast! We can see the pink slips coming right now!* When you are waiting for a miracle, God may tell you to do many things that may seem to be the opposite of a previous instruction. The question is this: Will you do what He says, even when it appears downright "stupid" to the natural mind?

If God asks you to awaken at 5:00 a.m. and pray, despite the fact that you crawled into bed only fours before, will you get up and pray? If He tells you to purchase a gift to bless the same employer who just cursed you and refused to give you a much-deserved raise, will you do it? If God requires you to "plant" your entire payroll check as a seed into a particular ministry, could you do it? Don't be surprised if God is preparing you and moving you into position to receive your miracle. Your pot is in position for a miracle, but it is *obedience* that moves you into position, fills the pot by faith, and delivers your miracle!

The miracle at Cana happened somewhere between the carrying of the cup of water by the servants and the tasting of the supernatural wine by the governor. It was during that short journey of absolute faith and obedience that Jesus stepped in and turned the water into wine! Is it any wonder that this transformation of the water of life into the wine of the Spirit marked the Lord's first miracle among men?

Chapter 4

From Scars to Stars

I was the third of 13 children, and the pressure was on to be "perfectly perfect in my perfection"! After all, wasn't I the daughter of a prominent bishop in a small town? Why couldn't I be as perfect as everyone expected me to be? I tried my best to please my parents and excel in the public school system, all while meeting the much tougher standards of the "wholly holy life" demanded of me by the "Who's Who" of my father's church. I struggled with the reality that I always seemed to fall short of perfection.

These issues, compounded by the normal stress created by the process of puberty for a young lady, pushed me to the edge of my ability to cope. I began to feel that no one was "safe enough" or "available enough" to understand my hurt, anger, and pain. One afternoon, I found myself sitting high above the hard oak pews of my father's newly-dedicated church sanctuary. Perched alone on the edge of the second-story balcony, I planned to commit suicide and "end it all."

Just as I rose to leap to my death, the back door of the church burst open, and a tall, 6-foot 3-inch man rushed into the sanctuary and fell on the altar in prayer! Who was this? *My God—it's my father, the bishop! What is he doing here?* I had counted on the fact that neither my father nor any of the church staff ever came to the church at that hour. He should be at home this time of day.

What should I do? I asked myself. I couldn't jump while my father was at the altar praying...I couldn't hurt him like that! Then the illogic of despair set in; I began to *pray* that my father would *stop praying* so I could kill myself! Ten minutes passed. Then 15 minutes and 20 minutes went by, yet my father was still there on his knees, immersed in earnest intercession. The bishop of the church, my father, prayed so long that as I hovered in the balcony, I decided to "hide" in the back corner to "pray" that he would leave. Then I began to remember all the little Bible verses I had learned throughout my long life of 13 years.

I remembered the little cards the Sunday school teachers used to pass out that had the pretty pictures of Jesus; the disciples; Mary the mother of Jesus; Jesus healing the sick, dying on the cross, and hugging and holding little children. Dad prayed so long that I began to remember the Bible verses that matched the pictures on those cards. I remembered that my Jesus would "never leave nor forsake" me, and that He "loved me with an everlasting love." I remembered that Jesus came that we might "have life, and that more abundantly." Gradually, those verses began to drown out the persistent voice of satan that kept saying, "Jump, jump! No one loves you, no one really cares! Jump—you will never please everyone. Jump!"

Finally, the voice of satan was totally silenced as the prayers of my father were heard by God. He prayed so long that I finally gained enough strength and courage to walk down the stairs of the balcony to join my father, the bishop, at the altar. Many years would pass before I could tell Dad that the prayers he prayed that afternoon literally saved my life. My mother didn't even know about it until years later after I had married and established my own home. The shame and fear I felt over my thoughts of suicide kept me from sharing the story publicly until 1982!

Your suffering is for another's benefit.

I was ministering at a retreat in Wilmington, Delaware, when the Holy Spirit suddenly spoke to my spirit, and said, "Stop, and give your testimony about suicide." I said, "God, please don't do this. There are hundreds of people here—don't make me share that story. They already think I'm crazy." (I should have known better.) The Lord said, "I want you to share that testimony."

Finally I obeyed and shared the story of my crisis on the church balcony as a young 13-year-old girl. Almost immediately, a woman began to scream in the back of the church. When they brought her up to me, she told me she had prayed that very day, "God, if You don't do something for me today before 3:00 p.m., then I'm going to drive my car into the Delaware River!" She said she had listened to me minister all weekend at the women's retreat, thinking, *She doesn't know what I'm going through! Look at her—she's got a husband and kids. Lord, she's got a ministry and she's happy!* Then she prayed, "Lord, please let her say something I can identify with to help me with what I'm going through."

As the woman talked to me, the thought kept running through my mind, *What if my pride and ego had won out? What if I had said, "No, God. I'm not going to tell that story. I don't want people to know that I was at the point of suicide. Let somebody else tell their story"?* God wanted me to learn that I wasn't just living for myself. Even my weaknesses and failures could bring glory to God and benefit others facing similar problems! I began to understand that when people are called of God, they will often be exposed to experiences that are designed to help them minister with power and authority to God's helpless, hurting, bound sheep. This is the divine principle I describe as "turning your scars to stars"!

> *Casting all your care upon Him; for He careth for you. Be sober, be vigilant; because your adversary the devil, as a roaring lion, walketh about, seeking whom he may devour: whom resist stedfast in the faith, knowing that the same afflictions are accomplished in your brethren that are in the world. But the God of all grace, who hath called us unto His eternal glory by Christ Jesus, **after that ye have suffered a while**, make you perfect, stablish, strengthen, settle you* (1 Peter 5:7-10).

The emphasis of this passage is on the last phrase that says, "after that ye have suffered a while, make you perfect, stablish, strengthen, [and] settle you." All of us have something in common: *we each have a problem.* Somewhere, somehow, at some point in your life, trouble has touched you! Whether you cried tears on the outside, or internalized your pain in inward bitterness, you still have a problem. Many of us don't always acknowledge or admit to our problems. Nevertheless, it is still a fact that we all have them.

Perhaps you aren't facing a doctor's diagnosis of cancer or a bankruptcy hearing, but it is certain that you have been hurt in your life. Somewhere in the parade of your life, you have been wounded and battered and, willingly or not, you're walking around today with your scars on display. We may not see any physical scars, but that doesn't mean a thing; they are still there.

The most detrimental, damaging, and painful scars cannot be found on the outside—they are on the inside. Unhealed, festering, and beyond the reach of most human healers and physicians, some of these scars are really just gaping wounds that bite at us and cause us to ache, hurt, and bleed around the clock without relief or comfort. Yes, we all have problems.

You are in the fight,
whether you know it or not.

The day you joined the Christian "band," you really signed up for battle! There is a battle going on between satan and God for the souls of men. Until satan gets the news that the war is over, you must be ready to fight! God says, "Fight the good fight of faith" (1 Tim. 6:12a). The Lord never tells us anything without also supernaturally equipping us to do it. It is time to put our toys down, put our security blankets down, and pick up our weapons. Whether you want to or not, there's a war going on and you will have to fight!

Now in every battle, somebody gets hurt.... Most of the participants in a war walk away from the battlefield with wounds, even the winner. In any case, only those who survive and get through the battle alive can come out and announce, "I have the victory!" If there is no battle, then there is no victory. If you don't go through anything, if you don't have to worry about anything, then you'll never have victory either! But those who endure and survive struggles, challenges, and troubles are *candidates for victory*. They can declare, "What I'm going through is going to set me up for victory!"

Since winners as well as losers come out of a war with scars, you need to cast all your cares upon Him; for He cares for you (see 1 Pet. 5:7). That means you can lay all your burdens, your hurts and wounds, and your scars upon Jesus. Now you can't give something away unless you first admit that you have it! It's like the person with a cold who declares, "I'm walking by faith and I don't have a cold!" between sneezes, while nasal mucous runs down his face!

Don't say, "By His stripes I'm healed," until you admit that you need healing! Before you give your cares to Jesus, drop your pride and falsehood. Pull the mask off your face and admit you've got a problem. You can't get help for your marriage until you admit to God that you are doing a poor job with it. He can't help your finances until you recognize that you need help.

Many times, God's solution to our problem begins the moment we recognize our problem. Some of us faithfully give our tithes and offerings, and the Lord continues to open up the windows of heaven. Yet as fast as He opens them, we close them back up with our bad habits! I was shocked to discover that I had all the habits and symptoms of an impulsive buyer after I took a close look at our family budget (I get tired of God "hanging out all my dirty laundry" in public, but He wants to help you get free too!).

I noticed that when pressures mounted up in my life, I would go and spend hundreds of dollars to make myself feel better. Then when the bill came, I asked everyone in the house, "Now who put those charges on this account?" When I finally came out of denial and accepted full responsibility for my ungodly behavior, I fell down before God in prayer. I lifted up my hands in surrender and told the Lord, "I repent for being an impulsive buyer." I must confess that it took me about 30 minutes to get my hands up because I didn't want to admit to my weakness. I knew my acknowledgment would force me to take responsibility for my actions.

The worst thing you can do is hide from the truth and pretend your weakness or scar isn't there. God knows what you are hiding, where it is hidden, and why you are hiding behind those "fig leaves" of deception. He knows what is buried in your private closet of shame. He can tell you every time you have stood in the church building shouting "Hallelujah!" while you were cursing in your mind. He sees beyond the innocent smile you give the sister in the church foyer, and He sees you secretly undressing her with eyes of lust. He knows the vicious jealously that lurks behind the trite compliments you throw out to other women in the congregation who are dressed more expensively than you are.

You can't fool God, so stop trying. First, accept the fact that since you are alive, you *have been* hurt in the past, you *are being* hurt right now, and you *will be* hurt in the future. (Now you can really appreciate the Lord's invitation to cast *all* our cares upon Him!)

> *The worst thing you can do is hide from the truth and pretend your weakness isn't there.*

If you insist on saying, "I'm not hurting at all. There is nothing and no one in my life that is hurting me. In fact, I don't let anybody get close enough to hurt me," then you are *really* hurting! Some people try to wriggle out of the truth by saying, "I don't have any friends who can hurt me. I don't let anybody get in my life because, you see, *it's just me and Jesus.*"

I have news for you: Jesus didn't create you to be by yourself. In fact, you're even sick of yourself. I think God's probably sick of you playing the "Lone Ranger." He made you to share your life and gifts with other people on the earth. That is why He created the Church!

Understand that your hurts are "messengers from satan" sent to buffet you, knock you around, or wound you (see 2 Cor. 12:7). Your hurts are assignments from satan. Now those hurts may come from satan, but the Holy Spirit of God is able and willing to turn them around. God wants you to say, like Joseph, "But as for you, ye thought evil against me; but God meant it unto good, to bring to pass, as it is this day, to save much people alive" (Gen. 50:20).

You also need to know what satan uses to wound and scar you. Paul told the Corinthian believers, "For we are not ignorant of his devices" (2 Cor. 2:11b). The enemy has agents strategically organized to attack the servants of God. They know when you are most vulnerable, but they just can't seem to understand how God works in us! God's Word says, "Ye are of God, little children, and have overcome them: because greater is He that is *in you*, than he that is in the world" (1 Jn. 4:4).

Satan uses your memory of hurts, failures, and sins from the past to entangle you in things that were washed away under the blood of Christ long ago. He will do his best to keep you from forgetting the past. He also uses the emotions of anger, grief, pity, and jealousy to sway us away from the truth of God's Word. He also uses sins of the heart like bitterness, envy, unforgiveness, and worry. Did you know that bitterness is sin?

Satan wants you to worry because it is a statement that loudly says, "My God isn't big enough to handle my situation." That is a trap from satan to make you think that you are equipped to handle a situation by yourself. He uses doubt to usher in unbelief; because when you stop believing God, you have signed your ticket to hell.

He uses doubt to create unbelief and produce one of his favorite emotions: fear. I have never seen so many saints running scared in my life. Believers are panicking over the economy, the anti-Christ, the liberals in government, and our crumbling position in world trade. What happened to God in this picture? Did somebody suddenly break His arm and steal His power? A lot of Christians are sure acting like it.

The enemy also likes to use hatred. He loves to create friction and foster unforgiveness in our relationships, hoping we won't resolve them, because then he can start planting hatred in our hearts. When you hate somebody, you don't even have to see him; all it takes is for someone to mention his name and you start your fussing! The enemy especially likes to sow discord among friends in the Body of Christ.

Sometimes the devil uses the divine acts of God to wound you. If your mother goes home to be with the Lord, the devil will use it to make you bitter rather than allow you to rejoice. He wants you to say, "God took my mamma." Or God may be setting you up for a better job, yet you get upset because you were fired suddenly without notice. We must learn—in the midst of our pain—to be quick to praise God but slow to complain about our state.

Learn to recognize the tactics of the enemy.

If God wanted to walk you to the supermarket at a certain time to meet somebody in the parking lot who would offer you a double-paying job, what would happen if your were too busy cussing and fussing at God in your living room to even step out of the house? Is it God's fault, or yours?

The solution to every problem is your faith in God, and faith without works is dead (see Jas. 2:26). Faith is the opposite of fear. Although it is the nature of fear to cripple, the nature of faith is to heal and strengthen. Fear blocks; faith opens up. Fear locks up, but faith moves out and against. Fear brings doubt, but faith brings belief. Fear wounds you, but faith heals you. Fear scars you, but faith transforms your scars to stars!

> *There hath no temptation taken you but such as is common to man: but God is faithful, who will not suffer you to be tempted above that ye are able; but will with the temptation also make a way to escape, that ye may be able to bear it* (1 Corinthians 10:13).

Deal with your problems, hurts, headaches, tears, fears, and worries through faith. Jesus said, "I will never leave thee, nor forsake thee" (Heb. 13:5b). If Jesus is always with me, forever and ever; past, present, and future; then He was with me when I got hurt too. He was right there when you were beaten and knocked around by the enemy. Jesus was there all the time. He felt what you felt, and He knew what you were going through. Before it became more than you could bear, He stepped in and said, "Satan, back off. I have promised not to allow you to put more on My children than they could bear."

"If Jesus was there, then why did I have to go through this problem at all?" You had to go through your problem because there's no more room for the great examples of faith in Hebrews 11. From the beginning in the garden, God in His unmatched wisdom, knew that people in the late twentieth, and twenty-first centuries would not want to read their Bibles like they used to. Today, people don't read Bibles—even Christians! Our generation seems bent on preparing "jet saints" for the "jet age," but God says, "I am going to anoint some of you with the ability to become *living epistles*. People may no longer read the Word of God, but they will read your life!"

Somebody has to go through financial struggles, identity crises, loneliness, alcohol and chemical addictions, eating disorders, terminal illnesses, and "sexual orientation" disorders. Why? So God can bring them out with bold, irrefutable testimonies to His glory and faithfulness! As we go through our everyday promises, experiences, challenges, and struggles, the world will see some of us fall. They will see some of us become disappointed, hurt, and angry.

The good news is that if they keep watching, they will see the truth in Proverbs 24:16, which says, "For a just man falleth seven times, and riseth up again...." If the world keeps on watching, they will see Jesus pick us up, brush the dust off of our backsides, and set us on the road again. The world will see God take the crooked things in our lives and make them straight. People will see God take the darkness out of our lives and make it light! They will see God make a hopelessly depressed woman full of joy for a lifetime. They will see God take a drunk who is stumbling into his house come out with his hands surrendered to Jesus. People will see God in your life if you are willing to pay the price to become a living epistle!

God is sick of hearing His people talk about their miraculous God with one breath on TV, radio, and in Christian magazines and books, only to turn around and swap wives with their elders or pick up a "new spouse" down the street. If God truly is a miracle-working God (and He is!), then He is well able sustain our marriages, put in order what is out of order, and keep us restored in His joy! The problem is that nobody wants to become a living epistle. Nobody wants to stand in faith long enough for God to transform their scars into stars!

The world needs living epistles to read.

The only way for the world to know the glory of God and see that He does work miracles is for it to happen *through* you! We need to stay in the battle long enough for God to turn our scars into stars! We need to stand in the same kind of faith as those who went before us "who through faith subdued kingdoms, wrought righteousness, obtained promises, stopped the mouths of lions" (Heb. 11:33).

God won't have a reason to close the mouth of a lion in your life if you never get thrown in a lions den for daring to obey Him. He has no reason to cool you off in a fiery furnace unless you get some heat for refusing to honor men above God. The Lord has no reason to say, "I'll supply all your needs" unless you allow Him to do that by daring to defy satan's lies by tithing and giving to God in the face of some difficult financial crisis!

Too many of us want out of the fire, out of the den, and out of the grave too soon! Some of the things you will face in this life can actually kill your hope, your vision, your dreams, and even your desire to live if you have not learned to trust Him implicitly! I guarantee that if you haven't been there already, then you're on your way right now! The wisest thing you can do, as a blood-washed believer, is to stand on God's Word and submit to some trials and tribulations to see if you're really going to let Jesus fix your problems.

It is a little too late to pull out the owner's manual to look for the parachute section when your plane is falling out the sky. No, you want to enter the battle with tested and proven weapons and skills. When the fire comes in your life, when the problems and fear hit you in the night, you need to know where your fire extinguisher is. You need to know where to find the light. You need to know the number to call for help, and how to find your way to safety in the dark.

The Bible makes it clear that you are not battling against any man, woman, or beast. You aren't even fighting against a government agency or economic trend. There is no need to get angry at a supervisor, landlord, husband, or wife. You are at war with satan, the father of lies, who has inspired your own personal hell.

You need to know how to use the weapons that strike the most fear in your enemy—weapons like the sword of truth, the shield of faith, and the breastplate of righteousness. When sickness hits your body and tries to kill you, faith says, "No—hold it back!" When your heart is close to breaking, God says, "Don't worry about your heart breaking; I am the great Heart-Fixer." When you are so broke that you don't have a budge to budget, God says according to your faith, "I will personally supply all your needs." You need to tap the spring of life and power in the promise of God that declares to all the world and the dark world of fallen angels:

And He said unto me, My grace is sufficient for thee: for My strength is made perfect in weakness. Most gladly therefore will I rather glory in my infirmities, that the power of Christ may rest upon me (2 Corinthians 12:9).

What does it mean to have your scars turned to stars? I heard a story about a registered nurse at a hospital in Orange County, California, in the Los Angeles area. Everyone who came into contact with her noticed that she seemed to have an extraordinary ability to deal with hurting people. She just knew how to give hurting people shots and how to soothe them, and to speak softly at night so they would finally sleep despite their pain and discomfort. Time and again, people would say, "Boy, that is an unusual nurse." The head doctor on call explained why this nurse was so unique: "Yes, she is extraordinary. You see, she has been at death's door three times herself! It is because of her own painful experiences that she has learned how to minister to others in their pain."

What have you learned in your experience that will make you strong enough to help pull somebody else out of theirs? There is no scar in your life that cannot be made into a star in God's hands! If you want God's attention, however, then even though you are hurting, you must lift those hands up in spite of your tears and start to praise Him! When you praise God in the midst of your struggle and trouble, you quickly capture the loving attention of God! If you want to see scars turn into stars, you will have to get a fighting mentality! Take off those cute shoes and put on some combat boots! Buckle on your breastplate, slip on your helmet, and unsheathe your sword!

God is doing a new thing, and He wants to start with you! It doesn't matter what you've been struggling with, or how ugly your past may be. You are dealing with the Almighty God. He is out to heal and bless you right in front of your "enemies." He is going to restore you right in front of the ones who have abused you, and then He will anoint you to deliver them and bring them into the Kingdom too! But that can only happen when you are willing to pay the price to see your scars turned into stars.

Chapter 5

Rest in Stress

He healeth the broken in heart, and bindeth up their wounds (Psalm 147:3).

One of the most difficult things I ever had to do was to declare bankruptcy. I was attending Pepperdine University full time in pursuit of a graduate degree, and my husband was a full-time student at Cal State Fullerton. Two babies had been born during those years, and both of us worked to pay the bills. Then I had an unexpected bout with cancer. As the medical bills mounted, our chances for financial survival dwindled away to nothing.

When I sought the advice of a corporate attorney at the company I worked for at the time, he strongly urged us to file bankruptcy for the sake of survival. My husband was devastated. Both of us had been taught that biblically, we are required by God to "owe no man." Against our will, the financial pressures and stress kept growing to the point where we were pushed into bankruptcy court.

What a blow! We felt we had to hide our situation from both our family and our friends. We didn't want anyone to know that we had failed financially. Somehow we managed to carry on our lives without anyone discovering our secret. Then God stepped in.

Suddenly, Wayne received the call of God to pioneer a new work in inner-city Los Angeles! We moved the work to Inglewood in its fifth week, and in our newfound success, we asked God, "How could this be? Would and could You use a couple who have failed financially and allow us to become stewards of Your funds?" Would we ever be in a financial position to purchase church facilities? How could we rest in such stress?

We learned that not only would God restore us financially, but He would enable us to pay *full restitution* to *every account listed on our bankruptcy* within two years! Despite our poor credit rating as "bankruptcy filers," we were able to purchase our first church site after just 12 months as pastors!

The miracles weren't over. Six months later, we miraculously purchased our first home and became living witnesses and epistles to the power of faith in the midst of poverty. Over and over again, we encouraged other couples to know the God who was willing and able to restore, regain, and recoup all their losses—if they would put their trust in Him.

There are times when God calls upon you to minister from your own personal experience. Daniel's testimony was great for his day and time, and Job's testimony stands as an example for all time; but in this year, in this moment, we each need our *own* testimony proclaiming how God has moved on our behalf. If God can't wipe my tears when I'm crying, then don't tell me that He wipes away tears. I don't need a God who is only an abstract theory out of someone else's mouth. I'm thankful that I serve a God who meets me where I am.

God will call you to minister from your personal experience.

It is only by identifying God's hand in our lives that we can learn to rest in our stress. Stress is the result of a broken heart. I know we like to cover up the truth with all the symptoms and circumstances that work together to produce the stress; but whether you say your boss laid you off, your husband left you, or your kids are acting up, it all boils down to this: Stress is no more than the sign of a broken heart. You have set your heart on something that has been broken in your sight. Your heart has been broken by a demonic force, by worries and cares that originate with satan.

If you are saved, then you are the devil's enemy. He hates you. Your unsaved employer may treat you well on the job, but the bottom line is that you are saved and he is not. The spirit of satan that rules him may rise up against you any day in rebellion against the spirit of God at work in you. Satan works through our own weaknesses, through other people, circumstances, and things to express his hatred toward the Kingdom of light. Since he is greedy beyond measure, once he feels he has an advantage, he will press the situation so forcefully that even the most spiritually nearsighted among us can recognize his evil hand at work.

When my two daughters were in their teens, we had just purchased new carpeting, drapes, and special furnishings for our new home. We spent $20,000 before it suddenly dawned on us that all the bills for these purchases would be due and payable within 45 days! We held a family conference to find creative ways to pay all our new debts. After much discussion, I suggested that I sell my automobile and share cars with my daughter, Wendy. This was rejected. Then I got especially "deep and spiritual" (confession time again) and suggested that we contact a bank or lending agency for loan. However, God had a special answer and "instrument of rebuke" for my "spiritual" suggestion. At that moment, my youngest daughter, piped up with the comment, "But, Mom, we can't get a loan because Daddy preaches that 'we shall lend to many nations and borrow not'!" Naturally, I wanted to pop her in the mouth, but I suddenly realized that the Lord was speaking through my little girl. We all repented and immediately asked God for His wisdom.

Each day after that, I prayed and praised God for meeting all our needs according to His riches and glory. It was right in the middle of this time of "stretching and pulling" of our faith to meet our financial obligations that our neighbor's dog began barking loudly at 3:00 one morning. A trio of young men were trying to break into our brand-new Cadillac. As they shattered the glass and prepared to enter the vehicle, the dog's owner, a California Supreme Court judge, awakened and called the sheriff's department.

Three days later, we were sitting at the breakfast table having breakfast when we heard a loud crash. We rushed outside to see a U.S. Postal Service jeep jammed into the rear of my daughter's beautiful blue and white Reliant. Two days after that, I was taking my two daughters to dinner in our only undamaged vehicle after a long 12-hour day at the church when a truck suddenly careened out of nowhere at an extreme rate of speed and crashed into us! The driver looked quickly into our faces and then sped off! We were left there in a damaged vehicle, victims of a hit-and-run driver. We praised God that we came through it unhurt.

What was going on? Now we had $20,000 of immediately payable debt and multiple insurance filings in progress. The young men who had attempted to steal our car were found, and when we appeared in court for prosecution proceedings, we discovered to our amazement that the ringleader was the son of a Pentecostal pastor in a nearby community! How do you prosecute the son of a fellow minister in the faith? Since so many other cases were brought against him, the matter was taken out of our hands. We were given the privilege of replacing our car with a new Cadillac because the damages from the attempted theft were so extensive. Somehow in that process, we were given a refund check for $10,000. This was "miracle number one"!

One week before the balance of our decorating and furniture bills were due, the Postal Service paid the damage expenses for Wendy's car. The final miracle illustrates just how important it is to be obedient to the will and voice of God no matter what! Three days before we were struck by the hit-and-run driver, God spoke to me and said, "Call your insurance agent and make sure that you have uninsured motorist coverage." I immediately secured that coverage on each of our cars. Little did I know that when the accident with the hit-and-run driver occurred, it qualified me for restitution under that policy.

In the end, we recieved $10,000 from the the attempted theft of the Cadillac, approximately $1,000 from the Postal Service, and more than $15,000 from my insurance company—all in time to pay every debt.

---

*When you identify God's hand
in your life, you can rest in stress.*

What appeared to be unsurmountable stress turned out to be unsurpassed blessing as I learned to *rest in stress*! I know that many of us like to think that since we are in Christ we will never have anymore problems. We like to think we will be smiling every day. I'm sorry to bring you bad news, but Paul warned us, "Yea, and all that will live godly in Christ Jesus shall suffer persecution" (2 Tim. 3:12).

No, you cannot prevent your heart from being broken, but *you can control the destiny of how you come out of your brokenhearted situation*! Your destiny depends on whether you give it to God or not. If you cling to that broken heart, pet it, and rub it, then you will nourish the pain; and it will destroy you. If you allow the pain of what you're going through to become your focus, your heart will never heal. God has the power to heal your broken heart, but you must give it to Him, lay down, and rest. This is a job for God, not for man.

Stress is an enemy force that must be mastered. It can severely damage you and your relationships if it is not mastered. Stress will make you bend over and walk like you're 90—when you are only 22 years old! Stress will make you hold your head down, and if the right degree of stress hits you, your mind will make you roll up in a ball and sleep in a fetal position in a desperate reach for the security of your mother's womb. Stress will push you back to the earliest stages of your development and make you hide from the pressures of life.

Stress is something that the devil brings when he sees he can't get your body. He simply moves to another playground in your life; he reaches for your mind. The number one disease in the United States is stress! How many times have you been to a doctor, talking about how your stomach hurts, your back hurts, or your head hurts. The doctor diligently takes x-rays, sticks you with needles, and prods, pokes, and thumps you every which way—all to show you what he already knows—there is absolutely nothing physically wrong with you. They don't want to tell you that they think you're crazy because they know what you are *feeling* is very real.

We have to learn to *give back what is not ours.* Too many times we try to do God's job and fail miserably. Other times we are gullible enough to accept the devil's gift of sin, sickness, or sorrow. They all produce stress, but stress is only a phase. Anything the devil does is only a phase because everything passes away but the Word of God. The devil is not the Word, so whatever he does is going to pass away. It won't last, for this too will pass. Don't tell God, "I can't take it anymore" because God took it for you. So give it back to Him and go ahead with life as He has always intended.

Stress is just a phase.

One time, my zeal and presumption created some painful stress (and embarrassment) in my life. I had to learn that miracles don't "just happen," and that not every miracle I am "believing God for" will happen exactly as I envision it.

Wayne and I were believing God for a new church edifice. We had raised the money for the down payment, and all that was left was for our banker...pardon me, *for God* to guarantee the loan for the balance. I have to laugh when I think of it now, but for a long time it was a painful memory. "By faith," I had the church put a big article in the local newspaper describing our upcoming purchase and thanking God in advance.

You can probably guess what happened. The loan fell through, and we did not get the church building! I was heartbroken. I prayed, "God, what is wrong here? This is not a personal home purchase, and it is not for our own gain! This is for Your Kingdom! This is because the ministry You have entrusted to us has outgrown its present building. Common sense says that we need a new building."

Then I really got serious: "Come on, Lord. Let the loan go through. What is wrong with wanting a new building? With this new building, all the other churches and pastors will take us seriously! They will know that

You, God, have put us on the map. We're not just two kids trying to pastor...this will be big time stuff, for this is over one million dollars."

Much to my dismay, God still did not allow the loan to be approved! I was heartbroken again, embarrassed in the church community, and downright angry with God. I asked, "Lord, what is going on?" And He replied, "I don't care about causing you to lose face in the public's eyes, neither am I concerned about you becoming embarrassed. If what you want does not bring Me glory and honor, then I am under no obligation to perform it." (Wow, talk about a humbling moment....)

What I did not know was that God had prepared another building only one block to the north of the site I had set my own sights on. God was just waiting for us to acknowledge Him in all our ways. Suddenly, God sold us this building for half of its value, renovated it, and allowed us to move into it in just a matter of weeks, *without a bank loan!* God did not want us praising and thanking a banker, He wanted to give us a building that would create an atmosphere of praise and honor that would go entirely to Him!

You were born to be a witness. Think about it: Do they put people who haven't seen anything on the witness stand in courtrooms? How can I tell you that God can bring you out if I haven't been in a pit and let Him bring *me* out? The devil wants to make us think that just because we are a witness to his attack, that *we* are on trial! The witness is not the defendant—you are not the one getting sentenced; you are just the witness. God lets you walk through this life and experience a problem so you can give it to Him and *witness* His power to overcome it. It is the devil who is on trial for his hell-raising, home-breaking, marriage-wrecking, health-stealing ways. We are not here to be victims, we are here to be witnesses to the devil's lies and to God's glory.

I sometimes wonder if Lazarus was buried by his so-called friends a bit before he was "certifiably" dead—and all because of stress. The Bible says Jesus wept before His friend's tomb. Could it be that the Lord cried because everyone else's unbelief added to Lazarus' stress? Some of us have let the devil whip our heads and batter us so much in life that everybody thinks we're dead. They are busy preparing our funeral arrangements and picking out caskets when we're just suspended in a coma.

Don't let your stress become your friend.

You had better quit "playing dead" and wake up before you get hurt! I believe that since God didn't take Lazarus' life, He didn't put the stone on the grave. What did Jesus tell the men at Lazarus' tomb? "*You* move it" (see Jn. 11:39). Some of us have piled burial stones on people's lives and tried to seal them away forever...or so we thought! Sometimes, instead of being witnesses to the truth, we have moved into the arena of being *false* witnesses! Some of us are going to have to cut ourselves free of the stress and some of the mess that's in our lives, so we can receive something better.

Some of you are habitually depressed because you like your stress. You seem to like finding excuses to drag yourself around looking defeated. When you're faced with stress and pressure, just let the devil know that he can't control or stifle your life! Take your time and walk through this life as a victor, not a victim. Strut your stuff in the devil's face. Rest in that stress.

Don't let the devil dictate to you, just tell him where to go because you're "in the know"! Sometimes I think we wear the wrong shoes for battle. We need to stop putting on spiritual tennis shoes and fuzzy house slippers to fight our battles. Put on spiritual cleats like the cleats football players wear. We need to get some of those cleats, so that when we step down on the enemy, we will feel it! Every once in a while, put on some sharp razor cleats like baseball players wear. That way when you get ready to go into battle and run through the enemy's troop, your cleats will be grabbing some devil's nap! He's under your feet, so go for his head! He's already bruised, but add some insult to his injury!

One of the great dangers you face when you've been in or under stress for a long time, is that it becomes hard to turn loose because "it becomes a friend." You probably have one or two friends who you know are not good for you. If you were honest, you would admit that you really don't care for them yourself. Perhaps they get on your nerves, but they are "comfortable" to have around because you are familiar with them, and they demand so little of you. All they want is to attach themselves to you and live off of your life.

You know what to expect out of them, whether it be good or bad, and you just go along with the relationship because you're afraid of the "risk" associated with reaching out to new friends and the unknown. Some of you are so afraid of a life free from stress that you would rather hang on to the habit (and the odd security) of stress.

You already know what worry is like. You know what a headache is like. You know what heartache feels like. You made room for the lonely, biting companion called bitterness long ago. You would rather have these wearying but familiar companions than take the challenge to let them go and follow the winds of God to freedom. The truth is that the addiction to the fruits of stress—like depression, worry, heartache, and bitterness—is a habit that must be broken. The cure is sure: You must *rest in your stress*. Cast all your cares on Jesus, for He cares for you like no other.

Chapter 6

Stand in the Flames and Laugh!

My God, my God...please help me!

I had been married only a few months, and I had promised my parents that I would finish my college education. Transferring from the University of California at Davis to the University of California at Los Angeles was tough enough, but now I had to ride the city bus to my classes. And every morning when I got on that bus, I got sick.

"Oh God, please help me! Oh no, I'm throwing up again! That means no school today." I staggered to the nearest phone and called Wayne: "Please come and pick me up at the corner of Wilshire and Robertson Boulevard. I feel so sick, Wayne..."

A few hours later, I was sitting in the waiting room at Kaiser Hospital when a nurse called my name and escorted me to another room. Shortly after that, a doctor told me, "Yes, you have the 'flu'...but I'm afraid you won't get over it for another seven and a half months because you're *pregnant*."

"But I can't be pregnant! I am taking the birth control pill! Besides, I prayed." Oh my goodness, what did I *really* pray? Let me see...I prayed, "Lord, please don't let me get pregnant until after I graduate from college." The only problem is that at the end of the prayer, I remember saying, "Thy Kingdom come, Thy will be done."

"Okay Lord, what is going on?! It can't be Your will for me to have a baby just yet! Wayne wants to change his job, and we agreed that we would wait five years before having children so we could both finish school. Lord, there is no money or time for a baby!"

What seems destructive in our lives will often turn out to be a blessing in disguise if we trust God.

Finally, after all my protests and fuming, I began to submit to His gentle voice. "God, I don't understand it, but somehow, I must get through this experience. A baby is a beautiful gift from You. But am I ready? After all, just because I'm the oldest girl of 13 children doesn't mean I know what I should do as a mother..."

In the months that followed, I ate like a pig and gained too much weight (ballooning from 113 pounds to 180 pounds). A complication forced me to remain in bed for three months, as I noted in Chapter 3. It was 1969, and there wasn't much Christian television available in those days. My favorite pastimes became eating food and watching television. You can imagine what a mess I became! Spoiled, bratty, and fussy, I complained throughout the whole pregnancy until the eighth month when I realized that something wonderful, great, and exciting was about to happen! Wayne and Wanda, the newlyweds, were about to have a baby!

Sure enough, on the ninth of April, a beautiful baby girl was born, and we named her Wendy. The whole process repeated itself two and a half years later when, despite the fact that I had again consistently taken birth control pills, our second wonderful little angel was born into the world and was named Whitney!

Ten months after little Whitney's birth, I began to notice some unexplained hemorrhaging that wouldn't go away. By then I was working toward a graduate degree, and I thought, *There is just no time or money available for me to be sick right now!* After a while, I couldn't ignore the symptoms any longer. After two minor surgeries, just before the Christmas holidays, I was diagnosed with cervical cancer in the third stage of growth. In December of 1972, I underwent a major surgical procedure to remove my cervix. The procedure also left me totally unable to give birth to any more children. Then it dawned on me that April fifth would mark the *fifth anniversary* of my marriage to Wayne! If God had listened to us, we would have never experienced the joy of seeing our children born into this world! Through our stress, God intervened, and His perfect will superseded our selfish wills. In the end, we were blessed—even in our stress!

What seems destructive in our lives will often turn out to be a blessing in disguise if we rest in God. It is through the stresses of delays, denials, and redirection that God sets us up for wonderful experiences in life.

While I was recovering from the cancer surgery in my home, Wayne took the girls on to church one Sunday morning and let me sleep in to recuperate. I was sitting quietly in the living room when I suddenly noticed that I had begun to hemorrhage again. As fear tried to grip my heart and paralyze my thoughts, the words of Isaiah the prophet returned to my mind, "...with His stripes we are healed" (Is. 53:5).

I forced myself not to panic. I was determined to trust God for a miracle, despite my doctor's warnings about unexpected bleeding. Minutes later, the doorbell rang. It was Wayne and a guest evangelist who was ministering that morning at our church, Rev. Nealon Guthrie of Rome, Georgia. He walked in that door, pointed his finger in my face, and declared, "Though you be polluted in thine own blood, *live*, I say *live!*"

This prophecy, drawn from the unforgettable passage in Ezekiel 16:6, ushered the very power of God into our small living room that day! Once again I felt a miracle taking place in my body. I learned later that when Rev. Guthrie stood to minister, he looked over at the organ where I usually sat and asked, "Where is that little girl who plays the organ so beautifully?" When he learned that I was at home recuperating from cancer surgery, he asked to be taken to my home.

How wonderful it was to see Jesus walk into the personal moments of my life, interrupt satan's plans for my untimely demise, and surprise me with a miracle of healing and a promise of life in utter defiance of death! His presence gave me the power to stand in the flames of adversity and laugh at the devil's schemes. I could laugh "...for I know whom I have believed, and am persuaded that He able to keep that which I have committed unto Him against that day" (2 Tim. 1:12).

The enemy doesn't want you to forget the pain of your past. He works tirelessly to bring up vivid memories of every hurt, failure, disappointment, rejection, and embarrassment you have ever suffered! That isn't good enough—he also tries to get us to *anticipate* pain and sorrow *before it ever happens!* He will get into your imagination if you let him and spawn delusional thinking, which will affect your ability to make decisions.

Many young women who have been victims of physical or sexual abuse loudly declare they will never take that kind of treatment from a man again! Five years later we often find them in marriages to abusive men and the objects of weekly or daily abuse. They made decisions about a lifelong mate in the grip of delusion, thinking, *Well, he will be different. I can **change** him.*

The enemy doesn't want you to forget the pain of your past.

I'm sure the three young Hebrew men who were carried off to Babylon with Daniel were haunted by memories of what once was and what "could have been." They had many "reasons" to doubt God and turn away from Him. Yet they trusted God so much that when King Nebuchadnezzar threatened them with death in a fiery furnace if they refused to renounce God and bow to the king's image, they said,

> *...Our God whom we serve is able to deliver us from the burning furnace, and He will deliver us out of thine hand, O king. But if not, be it known unto thee, O king,*

that we will not serve thy gods, nor worship the golden image which thou hast set up (Daniel 3:17-18).

How could they do that, knowing they would instantly be thrown into the furnace? They had a relationship with God that went beyond scrolls, hymns, and rituals. The product of their faith was threefold: First, they were rewarded by being thrown into the flames. Second, they discovered that they weren't in the flames alone...

Then Nebuchadnezzar the king was astonied, and rose up in haste, and spake, and said unto his counsellors, Did not we cast three men bound into the midst of the fire? They answered and said unto the king, True, O king. He answered and said, Lo, I see four men loose, walking in the midst of the fire, and they have no hurt; and the form of the fourth is like the Son of God (Daniel 3:24-25).

Third, God received the kind of glory that can only shine forth from the manifestation of the miraculous in the eyes of unsaved and unredeemed men:

*And the princes, governors, and captains, and the king's counsellors, being gathered together, saw these men, **upon whose bodies the fire had no power**, nor was an hair of their head singed, neither were their coats changed, nor the smell of fire had passed on them. Then Nebuchadnezzar spake, and said, **Blessed be the God of Shadrach, Meshach, and Abednego**, who hath sent His angel, and delivered His servants that trusted in Him, and have changed the king's word, and yielded their bodies, that they might not serve nor worship any god, except their own God* (Daniel 3:27-28).

You and I were destined to stand in the flames of adversity and laugh! Why? Because we will never be alone in this world, or the next. We have an assurance that cannot be taken away:

Nay, in all these things we are more than conquerors through Him that loved us. For I am persuaded, that neither death, nor life, nor angels, nor principalities, nor powers, nor things present, nor things to come, nor height, nor depth, nor any other creature, shall be able to separate us from the love of God, which is in Christ Jesus our Lord (Romans 8:37-39).

When you get right down to it, there is only one being in existence who has both the authority and potential in the flames to remove you from the Lord's side, from His blessings, and from the covering grace in His Word. No, it isn't satan—he doesn't have any more authority in your life than the authority you give him. No, it isn't God. Although He has all power and authority, He does not have the potential or willingness to go against His own Word or character. Only one creature has both the power and the will to throw every good thing away on a whim—*you.*

I've found that most of the time, I am my own worst enemy. I remember the time I went away to a health retreat to "learn how to eat, rest, and generally take care of myself." After I "graduated," I started traveling and immediately got off of my diet and exercise regimen. I quickly pinpointed the culprits, of course. First, I blamed the hotels I stayed in. "They don't have the right kind of healthy food for me to eat," I complained to anyone who would listen. "Of course, I have to eat what they offer, so it's the hotel's fault that I'm off track." (Of course, once I came off the diet, my cholesterol count went up, my feet began to throb with poor circulation, I began to feel bloated and sickly—but I made sure everyone knew it was the "hotel's fault," *not mine*). Was I right? No, I was wrong! I could have chosen to fast rather than eat the wrong food groups.

The second culprit I blamed (less loudly) was my mother. I claimed that since I didn't want to offend my mother, whom we were visiting, I had to eat generous portions of her rich and delicious pies, cakes, and confections. Of course, I could have always gently explained to my mother why I must not eat her delicious pies and cakes. I was in a place in my life where I had to watch my diet to control cholesterol and saturated fats so I could live a long life and prevent disease. My mother's food wasn't my obstacle or opponent. My personal lack of discipline and lack of commitment to a difficult goal was the problem. I needed to point my finger away from the hotels and Mom; the problem was a little closer to home....

I believe that God has handpicked certain Christians (if not all of us) to believe and live out His Word on this earth in "living color." People of your community (both secular and spiritual) are focusing their gaze on you and what you do. Your relatives, your neighbors, your fellow employees, and your enemies may not read the Word of God, but they are reading your life with incredible attention to detail.

You must be willing to stand the stress of the test for your "readers." They need to see you take a stand for God even as you stare into the flames of the consequences of your statement of faith! They need to see you thrown into the situations that "try men's souls"! They should be pulled from their seats by the sight of seeing you standing and laughing in the same flames that have killed others. They should be so shocked to see the other Person standing at your side, the one with a form "like the Son of God" that they give God the glory!

> *The script of your life*
> *has been drafted by the Master*
> *for the "readers" He longs to heal.*

Somebody has to follow Jesus and carry a cross in front of the crowds in our own day! Somebody with a shepherd's heart has to go through the financial struggles just to show others the way, the truth, and the life that can be found en route to prosperity. Somebody must experience the crushing pain of an identity crisis and feel the loneliness and isolation of despair so they can point to the Answer, the loving Friend who sticks closer than a brother. Somebody with the mark of the cross has to experience the hell of alcoholism and chemical addictions to provide living proof that God is still the Deliverer!

Are you beginning to see that the text of your life isn't even about you? No, I'm not being harsh or insensitive. I'm saying that Jesus saved us so we could focus on something more important than receiving–*giving*. He called us to become like He is. He called us to lay down our lives for others. That is why He told His disciples, "If any man would come after Me, let him *deny himself*, and *take up his cross* daily, and follow Me" (Lk. 9:23). The text and script of your life has been drafted by the Master for the "readers" He longs to heal.

I can predict with authority that somebody in this climate of the nineties is ordained of God to struggle with "desires in conflict" en route to wholeness as a man or woman! Why? Because there are thousands of confused and wounded people out there in the death grip of bondage and past hurts. They have no idea what God intends a real man or woman to be or how they should act. God is about to raise up a scarred standard in the flesh, a standard of real, live, men and women who will bring Him all the glory!

---

*Wait on God and
let your "readers" discover
that your God is truly the Sustainer.*

The testimonies of Daniel, Meshach, Shadrach, and Abednego in their stand against King Nebuchadnezzar are recorded for benefit of their fellow Jews, and for every generation of Jews and Gentiles that would follow! The "script" of the Book of Daniel wasn't written for the benefit of the central players, it was written for the readers who would search their lives for evidence of God among very human people.

Can you see that the "readers" around you are examining every "word" of your life, too? They are turning the pages of your experiences in expectation, in the desperate hope that their search of your life will turn out proof of a living God! Their spirits cry out:

Show me that God is real! Please show me, tell me, prove to me that God is a deliverer! Make me to know that God can heal! I see you have been diagnosed with a terminal disease–so have I. But please don't give up in despair! I want to see how you survive your ordeal so that I can follow you too!

Wait on God and let your "readers" discover that your God is truly the Sustainer, that His name is *Jehovah-Rapha*, God the Healer! Your "readers" will be watching and observing you as you *go* and *grow* through the flames of adversity. Praise God for the glory that will come when you laugh in the flames, for your "readers" will also be there waiting when your God brings you out!

I believe that God purposely raises up believers who have endured, or come out of, every evil sin, plague, and vice common to their generation. That is why I am so sure we will see more and more "Holy Ghost survivors" emerge from the twisted remains of broken marriages, shattered families, and all the dark forms of abuse: verbal, physical, sexual and even "controlled spiritual abuse."

While the world is devaluing the marriage covenant and mocking all the things God calls holy, special, and wonderful, God is raising up scarred believers who will dare accept His Word concerning those who have fallen into sin and failure. (This is such a powerful instruction that I wish to share it with you first in the King James Version, and then in the Amplified Version.)

So that contrariwise ye ought rather to forgive him, and comfort him, lest perhaps such a one should be swallowed up with overmuch sorrow. Wherefore I beseech you that ye would confirm your love toward him. For to this end also did I write, that I might know the proof of you, whether ye be obedient in all things. To whom ye forgive any thing, I forgive also: for if I forgave any thing, to whom I forgave it, for your sakes forgave I it in the person of Christ; lest Satan should get an advantage of us: for we are not ignorant of his devices (2 Corinthians 2:7-11).

So [instead of further rebuke, now] you should rather turn and [graciously] forgive and comfort and encourage [him], to keep him from being overwhelmed by excessive sorrow and despair. I therefore beg you to reinstate him in your affections and assure him of your love for him; for this is my purpose in writing you, to test your attitude and see if you would stand the test, whether you are obedient and altogether agreeable [to following my orders] in everything. If you forgive any one anything, I too forgive that one; and what I have forgiven, if I have forgiven anything, has been for your sakes in the presence [and with the approval] of Christ (the Messiah) to keep satan from getting the advantage over us; for we are not ignorant of his wiles and intentions (2 Corinthians 2:7-11 AMP).

When men and women pay the price to become living epistles and exercise God's power in their lives and marriages, we will see our homes, communities, and churches strengthened! Part of the price of discipleship is doing whatever is necessary to learn how to overcome the "wicked one" and rest in stress. Satan is taking advantage of husbands and wives in the Church because we are *ignorant of his devices*! We have forgotten the warning of Jesus that satan, the thief, "cometh not, but for to steal, and to kill, and to destroy" (Jn. 10:10a).

*As we consciously decide
to live out the Word of God
our marriages and families become
strong, vibrant, and full of vitality.*

What better place could the devil target than our homes and our marriage relationships? Only as we make conscious decisions to live out the Word of God will our marriages and families become strong, vibrant, and full of vitality. It will require patience and the willingness to suffer without complaining. It will require dedication, which could amount to countless unselfish hours, weeks, months, and years of contribution to quality caring one for another. It will also require obedience, not selective obedience (which isn't obedience at all), but *total submission* to the will of God in our lives. It is then that we can stand together in the flames of adversity and laugh in the devil's face.

The world won't know this can be done until they see it done through you! You have to see the course through. You have to hang in there because a lot of people are basing their hopes on your trust in the invisible God. If you have to cry along the way, do it. Even Jesus wept and agonized at times. The battle may grow too intense and hot at times, but learn how to rest in His shadow and then get back in the fight. You have got to stay in the battle long enough for God to turn your scars to stars! Like the three

Hebrew children, and countless saints before you, you have to earn the right to stand in the flames with your Savior at your side and have the last laugh!

Who through faith subdued kingdoms, wrought righteousness, obtained promises, stopped the mouths of lions (Hebrews 11:33).

When you land in the flames, remember that "...faith is the substance of things hoped for, the evidence of things not seen" (Heb. 11:1). Your belief may get shaken and your circumstances may get rocky, but hold on to your hope in God. Things are about to change. You can live several days without food or water, but you cannot exist one minute without hope!

One of the positive things about stress is that it drives you to God. It is in the heat of the furnace that you discover you don't have to wait until you "get on your knees." In the few brief moments between your words of holy defiance and your leap into the flames, you will discover the secret of praying without ceasing! If the right trouble hits your house, your mind, or your body, every thought of fatigue will disappear in the face of a more desperate need to pray night and day! You will start speaking in tongues so much that you'll think you wrote the book on it! It is in those earnest moments of raw prayer and vulnerability before the Spirit of God that you will behold His face and be transformed. It is there, in the light of His presence, that He will join you in the flames and provide guidance for another day. It is then that you will feel a victory laugh rumble up through your spirit and ring through the flames of the furnace to the "readers" looking from the outside in!

Chapter 7

One Moment, Please

I felt like a passenger dashing through a crowded airport with everything in place—I had my boarding pass in hand, my seat had been preassigned and my bags were already checked. All I had to do was board the plane and take off for my destination.

Wait a minute...I thought I heard my name blaring over the loudspeakers.... **"One moment please**—*may I have the attention of Wanda Davis. There has been an emergency...please return to the ticket counter immediately!* **Your plans have been changed!"**

Early in my day, I was cooking in the kitchen when I suddenly felt extremely nauseated and fell to the floor holding my head. I crawled to my bedroom and tried to call my office staff for help, but when every effort failed, I turned my face to the wall and asked God for help. I desperately wanted to understand what was happening in my body!

Then the Lord spoke to me and said I was to intercede for the life of my husband—because he was facing a life-or-death trauma! I immediately began to pray in the spirit with deep groanings and agony. Shortly thereafter, the phone rang and the voice on the other end asked me to come immediately to the emergency room!

Oh God, I thought, *What could have happened?* Although I suspected the call was about Wayne, I couldn't help but wonder, *Is it my children? Did something happen at the office? What about my parents, are they well? What is going on?* Suddenly all my plans had changed. Just seconds ago, everything was set. Everything was perfect. All was well. I felt great; our money situation was fine; the family was super! Yet in one fateful moment a single, abrupt telephone message had shattered my world and brought everything crashing down, down, down! *God, please help me...!*

When I walked into the emergency room and saw my husband's battered body, I began screaming hysterically. I distinctly remember Wayne somehow reaching out with his bloody hand to cradle and comfort my hand in his as he whispered, "If you can take it, I can take it." In that instant, I felt the power of God dry my tears and strengthen my heart for the difficult task ahead. *We were in the flames again.*

As I looked at Wayne's bloody face again, the Holy Spirit brought to my remembrance a long-distance telephone call we had received from Pittsburgh just that morning. The caller was a young lady who had placed the call from a roadside phone on the Pennsylvania Expressway. She said she had been instructed by the Lord to "Tell Wayne Davis that I, the Lord, love him; and no matter what happens to him this day, remember that I, the Lord, love him!"

After Wayne had been wheeled away into an emergency treatment room, I sat alone in the swirling confusion of the Emergency Waiting Room at the Los Angeles County Hospital. The frantic ambulance crew had transported my husband there after picking up his body at a crime scene where he had been brutally beaten and robbed. Our Mercedes had been stolen, and my husband's body had been severely damaged.

Doctors were gravely concerned about the gaping wound he had suffered on the back of his head. For some reason they couldn't seem to stop the bleeding. His bruised hands were so swollen that our wedding ring had to be cut off his finger. I learned that our family physician was out of the country; but once he was located, he immediately instructed the hospital personnel to transport my husband to a local private hospital in Los Angeles.

When I looked at my husband as they prepared to load him into an ambulance for the second time that day, I realized that his mouth had been beaten so badly he could no longer speak. Wayne had swallowed some of his teeth, and his jaw was terribly swollen. *My God...could this battered piece of flesh actually belong to my husband? Lord, where are You? What is going on?* My emotions began to rise and I felt myself slipping, then I suddenly remembered the young woman's timely telephone call from Pennsylvania. Once again reassured of the Lord's abiding presence, my emotions stabilized immediately.

In his haste to transfer my husband quickly to the other medical facility, the emergency physician had Wayne moved into the ambulance before he stitched his severe head wound. As we learned later, this error led to some severe repercussions for Wayne. Determined not to be separated from my husband, I begged the doctors and ambulance attendants to let me accompany Wayne in the ambulance. Once they granted my request, I settled into a narrow space near Wayne's inert body and began the long, slow, ride through Los Angeles traffic, praying and hoping for a miracle.

Halfway between the two hospitals in the middle of a crowded freeway, the paramedic suddenly signaled to the driver that there was a serious problem with the patient: "His vital signs have dropped and there is no heartbeat!" I sat there as if frozen in place, desperately pretending that I don't hear a word they are saying.

God this can't be happening! My husband is a pastor, not a policeman or a gang member. He is supposed to be at his office counseling people, not fighting for his life in an ambulance! He is supposed to be on his way home for dinner soon!

Lord, You remember...(sob)...that special "soul" dinner I prepared–with the greens, yams, macaroni and cheese, and short ribs. Oh, Jesus...did I turn the burners off on the stove before I rushed out to go to the hospital?

My God...what about my daughters? Who will pick them up from school? How will I explain this terrible crisis to them? Dear Lord, let me stay focused. God, please save my husband's life! Spare him for Your name's sake...

The ambulance had barely come to a stop at the hospital emergency entrance when medical aides threw open the doors of the ambulance and grabbed the gurney bearing my husband's battered body. Someone shouted,

"Take him to the third floor!" as they rushed Wayne out of my sight, and I was simply told to stay behind.

By this time, word had gotten out about the incident. Police detectives and uniformed officers were everywhere, asking everyone questions. Congregants and family members were starting to gather by the hundreds at the hospital, and it quickly became evident that the hospital security staff really wasn't prepared to handle this kind of emergency. The mayor of Inglewood was contacted, and he quickly helped to arrange special police protection for my husband and my family—just in case my husband's attackers didn't want him to live long enough to identify them. "Lord, what is really going on?" I prayed.

The confused days that followed brought a seemingly endless series of surprises, crises, and mercifully, *miracles*. If I ever doubted it, I learned that the Lord did, in fact, love Wayne Davis. On the third day of his unplanned hospital stay, corrective oral surgery was ordered for his battered mouth and jaw. Somehow, the anesthesiologist forgot to inject Wayne before the surgical procedure began. Throughout the lengthy procedure, Wayne was *awake and aware* of every pain and pressure on his tender gums and jaw! He opened his eyes and desperately tried to find a way to tell someone that no one had given him medication for the pain he already felt, let alone to anesthetize him for the surgery!

At the height of his panic and pain, the Lord spoke to Wayne and said, "Look into the face of the nurse holding your head." Wayne told me later that when he obeyed and dared to open his eyes, he realized that the nurse was a former member of our church! She was gently holding his head, and at that moment she appeared to Wayne as an angel. Wayne testified that she literally *snatched the pain from his mouth, jaws, and teeth*!

While Wayne was in the Intensive Care Unit we learned that the neurologist could not stitch up Wayne's head wound because too many hours had elapsed since he had sustained the injury. When he began to hemorrhage as a result, the family was brought together and told that if the bleeding didn't stop, the neurological team would have to operate, and it would be very dangerous. Prayer vigils began to bombard Heaven from all around the greater Los Angeles area and across the country. Within hours, the bleeding had miraculously stopped, and once again, God gave us strength.

Meanwhile, the news media was having a field day with the sensational aspects of the vicious assault on my husband. Allocations were aired, rumors were openly pandered as facts, and many harmful lies were spread that wounded our ministry and our family. In the midst of this crisis, God reminded me of a Scripture He had given to me repeatedly through different people—around the country and abroad. Again and again, people had approached me—even total strangers in other countries—to declare a "word of the Lord" to me as found in Isaiah 54:4-8:

> *Fear not; for thou shalt not be ashamed: neither be thou confounded; for thou shalt not be put to shame: for thou shalt forget the shame of thy youth, and shalt not remember the reproach of thy widowhood any more. For thy Maker is thine husband; the Lord of hosts is His name; and thy Redeemer the Holy One of Israel; The God of the*

whole earth shall He be called. For the Lord hath called thee as a woman forsaken and grieved in spirit, and a wife of youth, when thou wast refused, saith thy God. For a small moment have I forsaken thee; but with great mercies will I gather thee. In a little wrath I hid My face from thee **for a moment;** *but with everlasting kindness will I have mercy on thee, saith the Lord thy Redeemer* (Isaiah 54:4-8).

This text had been given to me as a "personal message from God" so often that I had begun to resent it! I finally became so hardened to this passage that when someone would walk up to me and say, "My sister, the Lord told me to tell you that His special Scripture to you is..." I would sarcastically cut them off and say, "I know! Don't tell me—it's Isaiah 54!" Wouldn't you know, it was this Scripture the Spirit brought to my mind when I sat alone at the hospital trying to understand this big time interruption of my life.

> *If we can get to the place where we can submit to "one moment's interruption," on the other side of that moment we will find joy unspeakable.*

Suddenly I knew what God was saying to me each time He had sent wonderful people in His body to preach, recite, and speak Isaiah 54:4-8 into my spirit over the past 12 years! God was warning, advising, and comforting me ahead of time with the good news that even while everything was seemingly going great, "I am going to interrupt you with the words, 'One moment, please.' But fear not; you won't be ashamed, neither confounded, nor put to shame. And you won't remember the reproach of thy widowhood any more."

Now I realize that God was prophesying to me even then that sometime soon after this I would become a widow! He was telling me not worry about it, because He was my "husbandman." He was my Protector, my Provider, and my Sustainer.

He was telling me in Isaiah 54:7 that for a "small moment" He would seem to forsake me, or seemingly disappear from me. I believe He was telling me, "The pain of life and the pain of your crisis and trouble will seem to overwhelm you, but fear not! It is just for *one moment, please.*"

---

*Death has to work in us
as born-again believers if life
is to work in our dying world!*

God will cause those who don't like you to acknowledge His presence in your life if you stand fast for "one moment." When Wayne was recovering from his beating, the Word of God shining through him in the midst of his pain brought tears to the eyes of a hardened, unsaved detective who said, "This is strange. We've never seen anything like this." God caused a man with a degenerate spirit who did not know God to lose sleep until he walked into the 77th Precinct in Los Angeles and turned himself in, saying, "I beat a preacher. I didn't know what I was do-ing. I'm sorry."

If we can get to the place where we can submit to "one moment's interruption," then on the other side of that moment we will find joy unspeakable. We will enjoy a har-vest of hope and peace that we would have never experi-enced had we not endured that moment's interruption.

Jesus Christ died to save the lost. He willingly sacri-ficed His own life for you and I. His supreme sacrifice of love took away our sins and traded His life for ours. This is the foundation of our relationship with the Lord. The sacrificial pattern of Jesus' lifestyle is repeatedly worked out in the lives of all those who are joined to Him.

We are pressed on every side by troubles, but not crushed and broken. We are perplexed because we don't know why things happen as they do, but we don't give up and quit. We are hunted down, but God never abandons us. We get knocked down, but we get up again and keep go-ing (2 Corinthians 4:8-9 TLB).

Death has to work in us as born-again believers if life is to work in our dying world! You have to die for some-body else to live. Although the devil may "press" against us for the moment; he cannot crush and break us. We may be perplexed and confused about why things happen as they do, but we shouldn't give up and quit! The devil will attack us wherever he thinks he has a chance for suc-cess. If he can't destroy your marriage, he will try to drain your finances. If he cannot assault you financially, he will try to make you think you're losing your mind. Yet Scrip-ture says "...in all these things we are more than conquer-ors through Him that loved us" (Rom. 8:37).

I'm glad that even when we get "knocked down" from time to time, through Christ we just get up again and keep on going! These bodies of ours are constantly facing death, just as Christ's did. So it should be clear to all of us that only the living Christ within us keeps us safe. We live under constant assault because we serve the Lord, but this also gives us constant opportunities to show forth the power of Jesus within our dying bodies.

Paul told the Corinthians, "Because of our preaching we face death, but it has resulted in eternal life for you" (2 Cor. 4:12 TLB). We are like Timex watches, the brand whose slogan used to say, "We take a licking and keep on ticking!" There is a high price to pay when you choose to preach the gospel and represent Jesus Christ. We may face death, but we receive eternal life. Every person who preaches or ministers a message of life has experienced death of some kind in their own life in order to produce that living message.

"...I hid My face from thee for a moment; but with everlasting kindness will I have mercy on thee..." (Is. 54:8). What is a moment? Peter wrote, "But, beloved, be not ignorant of this one thing, that one day is with the Lord as a thousand years, and a thousand years as one day" (2 Pet. 3:8). We measure time in seconds, minutes, hours, days, weeks, months, years, and centuries. It may be that "a moment" is like a minute.

Math isn't my forte, but God woke me up early one morning and told me to get my calculator so He could show me something special. He told me to write across the top of a piece of paper: Seconds, Minutes, Hours, Days, Weeks, Months, Years, and 1,000 Years. Then He asked me to figure out how many seconds would fit under each category: 60 seconds per minute; 3,600 seconds per hour; 86,400 seconds per day; 604,800 seconds per week; an average of 2,628,000 seconds per month; and approximately 31,536,000 seconds per year.

Then He asked me to calculate the minutes under each category: 60 minutes per hour; 1,440 minutes per day; 10,800 minutes per week; approximately 46,800 minutes per month; 525,600 per 365-day year; and 525,600,000 minutes in 1,000 years (without leap year adjustments).

After I calculated every column on the chart, the Lord said, "Now tell Me how many seconds there are in 1,000 years." I answered, "There are 31,536,000,000 seconds in 1,000 years (without adjustments for leap years)." Then the Lord pointed out to me that there are 8,760 hours in one year, more than 365,000 days in 1,000 years, and more than 52,000 weeks in 1,000 years. I asked, "Lord, why are You showing me this?" He replied, "I want you to make a conclusion about 'this moment' in which you feel I have forsaken you. I want you to look in My Word and consider the people before you who endured for 'a moment.' "

He continued, "You don't have to go too far beyond Jesus Christ to understand. Jesus was hanging on the cross, bleeding, hurting, and suffering for what men account to be six hours. It could have really been 21,600 "moments," or 360 hours, or 15 days. How do you know whether I was measuring the suffering of the Lamb as one day or 1,000 years?

"I have put some of My people through experiences and because they're in the second or the third year, they're upset. They don't realize that they are still in the same 'moment.' Look at My moment in the tomb for three days and nights. It could have been *3,000 years* that I spent wrestling the keys of death, hell, and the grave from the powers of satan.

"I defeated all the powers in the pit of hell just to save you. Daniel's moment in the lions' den could have been measured in years instead of hours," the Lord said. "Job's fiery trial could have gone on and on. Paul's shipwreck experience came when I was getting him ready to become a missionary to a new world. What have you been going through for the past two weeks?"

---

*Don't let your present pain rob
you of your expectation of a great future.*

When God showed me that one day could be 1,000 years, and 1,000 years could be one day, I repented for my complaining. I realized that I might be standing in the twenty-second or the twenty-third day, but it is still just a moment in God's eyes.

"For a small moment have I forsaken thee; but with great mercies will I gather thee" (Is. 54:7). When your "moment" is over, when your time of suffering and trial is over, God will gather you. I don't know if you have ever been in the bosom of Jesus, but there is a place close to his heart where it seems you can almost hear His heartbeat, where you are close enough to be warmed by His blood and body.

Some of us go into spiritual, physical, or emotional shock when a moment of suffering hits, because it usually strikes right on the heels of a tremendous blessing, or immediately after we have received a tremendous (and true) prophecy of what God is going to do in our lives. We need to look beyond our temporary moment of affliction.

God is getting ready to do some great things for you and through you. His Spirit is continually at work in you to bring a spring season into your heart. You will find yourself beginning to dream again, right in the middle of all the opposition in your life! Don't allow the pain of your present moment to rob you of your expectation of a great future! You don't have time to complain! It's time to stretch and reach forth for the blessing and promises of God!

Enlarge the place of thy tent, and let them stretch forth the curtains of thine habitations: spare not, lengthen thy cords, and strengthen thy stakes; for thou shalt break forth on the right hand and on the left; and thy seed shall inherit the Gentiles, and make the desolate cities to be inhabited (Isaiah 54:2-3).

God is putting believers in little towns that are dying out or haven't been developed. He is causing the saints to be the first ones to buy the homes, and he is raising up saints to become developers and entrepreneurs. It is wonderful to see that God is in charge of the real estate on *both* sides of eternity!

He is orchestrating miracles even while He is promising to do some great things for you in the future. He is setting you up for greatness, and He is going to lift you up and turn you around. God is personally working out the details and bringing the right connections into your life!

Notice what God says in Isaiah 54:4, "Fear not." Now why would He tell us not to fear? Aren't we supposed to be getting ready for a blessing? Look at the words that follow:

> *Fear not; for thou shalt not be ashamed: neither be thou confounded; for thou shalt not be put to shame: for thou shalt forget the shame of thy youth, and shalt not remember the reproach of thy widowhood any more. For thy Maker is thine husband; the Lord of hosts is His name; and thy Redeemer the Holy One of Israel; The God of the whole earth shall He be called* (Isaiah 54:4-5).

God called you "when thou wast refused" (Is. 54:6). Then He said, "For a small moment have I forsaken thee." What is the Lord talking about? "But I came to You and received You as Lord and Savior because they told me, 'The Lord is your Shepherd, you will not want. He'll never leave you nor forsake you. He will supply all of your needs. It is His good pleasure to bless you.' So what is going on?"

Don't fear. God has simply put you into a place of "interruption." He chose you from among everyone else around you, and He put your name on this assignment...*just for a moment*. Now this moment may be for more than a few days. It might run for 15 days, three years, five years, or seven years.

There were many times in my life when the only thing I could do in my moment of affliction was turn my head to the wall and cry out to God. I know it doesn't sound very attractive or glorious, but I can testify that whether I was dealing with terminal disease, sickness, pain, tragedy, or unbearable loss, God always answered my call *personally*. I discovered that, no matter how dark the valley of death may appear, my Shepherd is always with me, and He will see me through it into the light.

The devil follows a clear pattern when he realizes you are in one of those "moments" of affliction. Expect to hear this old lie enter your mind: "All God's promises of safety, security, and life eternal in the Bible is for everybody *except you*. Don't you see—God can't forget what you've done. Why if the person sitting next to you right now knew what you've done, they would move to another seat right in front of everybody!"

When you hear that old tale, it is time to take satan back to Bible school! Give him a dose of "personalized prophet" and say, "I refuse to fear, because God says in Isaiah 54 that I will not be ashamed or confounded! God says I will not be put to shame! God says I can forget the shame of thy youth, and He says the reproach of my 'widowhood' won't be remembered anymore. In fact, my Maker is my husband—yes, the Lord of hosts is His name, my Redeemer!"

> The strength of the Word of God in you shining forth in the midst of adversity bears great witness to those who do not know Christ.

All too often, Christians today measure how well they are doing by looking at what appears to be prosperity and the blessings of God. I submit to you that when you get to a place where God can trust the Word that He has put in you, then *He will cause you to become a real witness* by allowing you to be tempered or strengthened through a "moment" of trial and testing. For a "moment," it will seem like He has forsaken you, but after you pass through the flames of adversity with the Lord at your side, He will cause people to say, "God is with that person!"

True spirituality and character are only exposed in the midst of pressure. Coffee beans never become anything to anybody until they are roasted over a fire, ground and crushed into usable form, and exposed to boiling water. Only then can they produce a beverage to be served to the multitudes as a refreshment.

God has an entire generation of thirsty souls longing for a refreshing drink of hope, for reassurance that "surely there is a God in Heaven!" They won't find refreshment in prime-time television, movie theaters, pop culture, or by indulging their own desires. There is only one place to drink from the river of God on this earth: They must find someone with rivers of living water springing up within them. They are looking for the people whose scars have turned to stars of hope and freedom.

They are looking for you—they are looking for a people who have submitted themselves to the fire, who have willingly laid their lives down before the crushing force of trial and affliction in Christ's name and have yielded their lives to be poured out for the healing of the nations. But before you can heal them in His name, He must interrupt you for *a moment....*

Chapter 8

Power in Your Zero Hour

It was perfect! What better setting could God have provided for hurting, bleeding, tired, and wounded soldiers to recuperate? The Davis family had waited entirely too long to stop and take a break. With a sigh of relief, Wayne and I herded our two young daughters onto the United Airlines flight. Finally, we were headed for a wonderful family break in Hawaii. We were in for a treat! After an uneventful flight, we were excited when we deplaned at Waikiki Beach.

Only a few hours later, Wayne began to experience chest pains. Within two hours of the appearance of those first symptoms, he was checked into a cardiac care unit and I found myself following the hospital's financial administrator into a private room. I could barely pull my thoughts away from Wayne long enough to answer his question about insurance coverage. When I said, "We don't have insurance coverage," he quietly but firmly told me that I must be prepared to guarantee the cost of Wayne's medical care. Then he told me the cost could run from $30,000-$60,000!

After a pause, the administrator mentioned that if Wayne and I did not have the financial resources to guarantee his care, the hospital would be "more than willing to place a lien" on our beautiful family home—to guarantee that Wayne received the care he needed, of course. After I made a quick call to the mainland, our corporate attorney and church financial officer reassured the hospital that we were good for the bill. As the hospital staff continued to provide medical attention to Wayne. At that point, the doctors warned me that he might have to stay in the hospital 10-14 days.

As soon as I could be alone, I ran to the Lord in prayer: "Lord…I am already weary and tired. I'm overworked, over-preached, over-counseled… Lord, I just want to rest. I need Your help, Lord! I just can't handle this right now! My little girls are still young, and they need childcare at the hotel while I am looking after Wayne at the hospital! Help me, Lord. I have no one else to turn to."

That afternoon, I was blessed as the management and staff of the Sheraton hotel cooperated with me and assisted in a great way with the children. They helped us until my friend, Georgia, arrived with her daughter to watch the girls for me.

At the end of the second day of Wayne's ordeal in the hospital, I walked out onto the balcony of the Sheraton overlooking the ocean and began to praise God in spite of my hurt and pain. I asked God to reverse Wayne's medical symptoms of a heart attack, and I asked Him to let my young (and once vibrant) spouse return home well and whole, saying, "After all, Lord, Wayne is just 37 years old, and I know You have so many plans for his life."

While I was praying, crying, and praying some more out on the balcony, I happened to look up and see a rainbow! I remembered God's covenant in the Old Testament and the significance of the sign of the rainbow. In that moment, I took that rainbow displayed outside of my balcony to be my personal sign of the covenant I had with the Lord. With renewed strength and faith, I began to declare and decree miracles over my husband's life and over our finances. I didn't stop there; I went on to ask God to release miracles and declare His blessings over our lives as never before!

I was still standing on the hotel balcony basking in the warmth of the Lord and His fresh word to me when the phone suddenly rang. Picking up the receiver, I heard the voice of the cardiologist on the other end. With hesitation, he said: "Mrs. Davis, I don't know how to explain this...I know what we saw yesterday, but this morning all the tests have reversed themselves! We cannot find any cardiac damage! I know this sounds awfully strange, but it's true. We will help your husband get some rest and relax a little more. We will give him some medication if we see any symptoms of anxiety and depression, but other than that, we'll just have to release him. There is nothing wrong with his heart!"

That was only the first miracle. Miracle number two was on the way. When I visited the hospital's financial office to check Wayne out of the hospital, I was told that the church had *already wired sufficient funds to pay the bill!* Although I was physically exhausted and mentally depleted, I left that hospital on spiritual wings! My spirit and soul rejoiced because during my lowest hour through the Word, through praise and prayer, I was reminded by my Lord that I was His own covenant daughter. In His grace I went from weakness to overcoming power.

We all returned stateside from our long-overdue "vacation," which had turned into another disaster. I had to immediately assume all the church leadership responsibilities normally handled by my husband, and I didn't feel ready or capable to handle much more than my own survival.

Wayne had been ordered to stay out of the office and the pulpit for at least two weeks of recuperation. I slumped down in my chair at the office, still desperately in need of a *real* vacation—I was back at home and back at work because there was a need. I had just conducted a staff meeting, counseled three people, and was trying to take a break before going to preach at another church in the city (where Wayne had been scheduled to minister).

You and I are heirs to God's covenantal promises of power and strength.

Somehow I had to muster up enough strength and courage to stand before hundreds of people and declare that Jesus is all in all when all I really wanted to do was to go somewhere and hide! "Lord, what can I say to these people tonight—they need encouragement too. I am so heavy and burdened, I feel weak myself, how can I help them? I feel like I am at the end of my rope...this is really a zero hour!"

I had just finished the last words of that prayer when my office door suddenly swung open. When I looked up, the receptionist handed me a Federal Express package that contained a book written by Benson Idahosa called *Power for Zero Hours*! My dear friend, Carolyn Harrell, had enclosed a short note that said, "God told me to send this to you. You need it. *Don't worry about feeling weak…*God's strength will be made strong in your weakness. Hold your head up, read this book, and do the will of God!"

Carolyn's note and the anointed message in Benson Idahosa's book were a shot of energy from Heaven. That night, I stood before a crowd of people on behalf of my husband and preached in the power of Jesus, "Power for Your Zero Hour!" What was meant to destroy me had become a platform to minister to others and bring healing and health to the hurting!

You and I are heirs to God's covenantal promises of power and strength. We don't have any reason to walk around like spiritual and natural weaklings! Don't bow down to your circumstances! Don't bow down to the devil's lies and curses over your life and ministry. Don't bow to anything but God Almighty! Gird up the loins of your mind and tap into the power and strength of your inheritance in Christ. There is power in the blood—even in your zero hour!

God's Word says, "The thing that hath been, it is that which shall be; and that which is done is that which shall be done: and *there is no new thing under the sun*" (Eccles. 1:9). *If it's a new thing, then it's not a **true** thing*; it is not of God! And if it's true then it isn't new.

If you're tempted to think you are the only one who has faced your problem—don't, because you aren't. If you think your problem is too big, too twisted, or too complex for God to handle—don't, it isn't. If you think you have found a shortcut or an "alternative" route around trials, tribulations, and challenges in the Christian walk—don't, because you haven't. You need God's power for every hour, but especially when the time has expired on your clock and you are facing your zero hour.

Too often, we prance into church on Sunday morning looking cute. The brothers have on their three-piece suits with the tie and pocket hanky matching to a "T," and every hair is plastered into place. While the brother sports his best Pentecostal grin, the lady on his arm is dressed to impress! Every sanctified sister has on a hat and a silk dress or a fine linen suit, complete with the latest pumps and a designer bag "worth begging for"! They all have "apostolic grins" fixed on their faces that say, "Praise the Lord! Everything is okay!"

---

*If you're tempted to think
you are the only one who has faced
your problem—don't, because you aren't.*

On the surface, everything looks wonderful, but underneath that well-dressed look and carefully-controlled smile, hidden behind that walk of confidence, lurks the truth. If the truth was known, everyone would know that the brother or sister in the pew beside them is up against a wall! He or she is facing one of the most trying circumstances of his life. It's his zero hour—and he needs the power of God *now*!

When you are at your screaming point, don't give up! Don't give in or give out: Wait on the Lord, because He who laughs last will be the Lord! Paul told the Christians at Corinth, "That your faith should not stand in the wisdom of men, but in the power of God" (1 Cor. 2:5). If you want things to *be* right, it is important to talk right and look right. But your outward actions must reflect what is really happening in your heart. Unless the power of God is released into your circumstances, you will just be a "fixed-up," messed-up person. (That is also a good definition of a corpse in a funeral home.)

The power you need in your zero hour will *not* come from the wisdom of men, so stop looking for man's help because it is in vain. The power of God, on the other hand, works in the most hopeless of situations. He restores wrecked relationships, including marriages that have completely broken up on the rocks. He restores finances that are so low you can't budget them. He can heal and restore your body, even when it is so wracked with pain and so crippled no medical doctor can help you.

There is one physician who can take all cases. Doctor Jesus, the Restorer of all things, has the prescription for your affliction! One dose of His power is all you need! All real power comes from God, and from God alone. There is only one way to tap into that power: "Let us therefore come boldly unto the throne of grace" (Heb. 4:16a).

Drop your pride and drop to your knees. Admit that you cannot help yourself—now or ever! Come before your Maker confidently, for you are not a beggar but a *child of God*. Come expecting to receive because the Bible says, "And this is the confidence that we have in Him, that, if we ask any thing according to His will, He heareth us: and if we know that He hear us, whatsoever we ask, we know that we have the petitions that we desired of Him" (1 Jn. 5:14-15).

Think about it: Every time you pray *according to His will*, you have it! Now you may not see the manifestation immediately, but it is yours! Who else can promise a 100 percent return on your (prayer) investment every time you invest?

You will only get power to help you in your zero hour if you admit that you need help. Even secular counselors and government agencies have had to admit that people with addiction and abuse problems can't really receive or benefit from help unless they first admit they have a problem! God's Word tells us to "come boldly unto the throne of grace." What is grace? It is something that you don't deserve and can't buy. It is a gift from God.

It is at the throne of grace that you obtain mercy. Mercy is God's way of sparing you, or withholding the total measure of the punishment you deserve. It is a matter of the heart. God empathizes with us to the point where He would rather take the punishment Himself than give it to you (which is exactly what He did through Jesus Christ!).

You may be thinking, *I don't need any mercy because I've been walking with God since I was first saved 20 years ago.* Honestly, I don't have that kind of testimony, and I'm fairly certain that if you are really honest, you would admit that you don't either. There are certain circumstances in my life that would destroy me if I didn't keep a tight hold on the mercy of God. How about you? If it was up to me and my righteousness and if the devil had his way in my life, I would be on the devil's junk pile some-where. It was the mercy of God that made the difference. Satan would have destroyed me in my mother's womb if he could have had his way. But I thank my God who al-ways causes me to triumph in Christ (2 Cor. 2:14)!

> *You need to "know that you know" that God's power is fully available to you.*

There have been times when I felt so low that I didn't want to have victory. I didn't want to triumph. I just wanted to die and get it over with. I'm thankful that my God made me—He forced me; He caused me—to tri-umph! He reminded me of my part in our covenant, the part where I committed my life to Him. He reminded me that my life is no longer my own to waste or cast away. He took away the power of choice, so He could make sure I would live the *abundant* life!

We serve a God of immeasurable love. When you didn't even want to be saved, the Holy Ghost wooed you anyway! When you didn't want to go back to church any-more, when you thought, *I'll stay home today*, all of a sud-den you found yourself rolling out of bed. You rushed around to put on your clothes and head for the house of the Lord anyway. Why? It is because your God causes you to triumph by helping you do the things that are necessary for victory. He helps you to find grace in your time of need.

All power has a source. As a born-again Christian, you need to be absolutely certain of where your power comes from. You need to "know that you know" that God's power is fully available to you. It will calm the waves of every storm that threatens your life. When stormy days arrive—and they will arrive—you can say "Blow on, storm. Blow your hardest! My God's grace is sufficient for me and He is in control of you!"

Habakkuk the prophet said, "The Lord God is my strength" (Hab. 3:19a). That simple little phrase is packed with significance for anyone who is facing his or her zero hour. Those six short words are really declaring, "The Lord omnipotent, the Lord omnipresent, the omniscient God is my resident power." By *resident*, I mean "living in a place, to serve in a regular or full-time capacity."[1] The power of God is a permanent tenant within the "penthouse" of your temple!

It is reassuring to know that no matter who or what I face in my life, I can rest because God's power is available to me right here on planet Earth! It doesn't matter what I'm going through, God is going through it with me. I don't know about you, but the God in me is big enough, grand enough, and great enough to be my power for my zero hour!

Sometimes we are faced with deadlines that cannot be avoided. Rent has to be paid each month. The kidney transplant may be needed in 90 days or you will probably die. You can have three months to move or you will be evicted because your apartment is being converted into a condo. We call these situations emergencies, and we nearly kill ourselves wondering if and when God is going

1. *Merriam Webster's Collegiate Dictionary.*

to "show up." All the while, we want to break out of the bondage of fear, doubt, and unbelief that has arisen due to the pressure of the zero hour. It may seem to us that the clock is ticking down and there is no more time; we are facing a "zero hour experience."

The way to get through a zero hour is to face reality with faith.

Everyone will face a zero hour at some time. They come suddenly as the unexpected situations that test the very limits of our faith and endurance. They are bleak hours filled with dark and dreary moments when you feel like you are in a tunnel and can't get out. You can't see a light anywhere ahead to help you get through the pitch-black darkness. These are the lean seasons of life, the bitter winter seasons when life, growth, and all forward movement seem to come to a dead stop. This season sometimes seems to drag on beyond endurance, for nothing seems to be getting any better and you seem to be at a standstill. (The hardest part about it all is that you are at a standstill.) You may feel trapped in the maze of life with no way out. A zero hour experience can leave a nasty taste in your mouth because these experiences are not palatable or sweet to the flesh.

Have you ever gone some place only to discover you couldn't get back the same way you came? No matter how hard you look, you can't find a single side exit, backdoor, or any other passage marked "This way out." Did you ever have everything turn upside down on you, leaving you to wonder if you'll ever able to stand up again, while you continue to proudly proclaim that you are the head and not the tail, above only and not beneath (see Deut. 28:13)?

I've been there. I still remember the chilling sensation I felt when the devil whispered in my ear at the age of 13 and told me to commit suicide. Oh yes, I was filled with the Holy Ghost, and I had tongue-talking, God-fearing parents. My daddy was, and still is, a full-gospel preacher. But in that "*moment*" of teenage crisis, when the devil told me, "You're unloved: Your mamma don't like you, and your daddy don't want you. They pick on you at school because you dress differently. They mock you because you're trying so hard to talk and walk different—it isn't worth it! You should just end it all. Go ahead—jump." Many people hear that same spirit of suicide taunting and tempting them with the lie that their pain will all end if they will just end it all with one fatal jump, one poisonous sip, or a quick lethal injection.

You can always recognize this kind of talk. The devil only comes to kill, steal, and destroy. But praise be to God, our Master always leads us to life, green pastures, and still waters. His grace will arrest the hand of death over your life. You may be thinking, "Oh, I have lived far above all that. In fact, I've never had emotional problems."

My friend, there are more ways to commit suicide than by merely destroying the flesh. You may have made decisions that are the equivalent to committing spiritual suicide! Perhaps the devil whispered to you, "Here you are, a fine, eligible, single young woman going to waste.

Your biological clock is just ticking away. How long are you going to wait around for some fool of a man to find you? Why don't you just take charge of your own future?!"

Maybe you did take matters into your own hands and grabbed a brother. Perhaps you decided the talk show gurus were right, that you were really born a homosexual. You may have taken other equally serious matters into your hands. When you impetuously walk out of the will of God, you have made a decision that can utterly destroy you spiritually. If you are not for God, then you are against God. There is no "middle ground." When God says, "Don't say it," you say it. When God says, "Don't go there. Touch not the unclean thing," you go anyway. Although God says, "Flee fornication," you jump into the next available bed you can find. That is *spiritual suicide*. Are you still able to say you haven't ever had any emotional problems?

Severe illness will quickly drive you to your zero hour. I was only 23 years old when they told me I had cervical cancer in its third stage! There were only two stages left! I had an 11-month old baby, another little girl approaching her third birthday, and a young husband that I loved dearly—now how would you feel if you were in my shoes and faced with a verdict like that hanging over your life?

You know you are facing a "zero hour" if you are still in the middle of making all your exciting plans for living and a doctor walks into your room to tell you that you have an advanced stage of cancer; and by the way, he doesn't know if they got it all during the surgery. In the agony and the desperation of times like this, many people can only shout in anger, cry, and moan, thinking that God has forgotten them.

The devil would like to see you face your zero hour and put your hands up in surrender! He wants to hear you say, "Stop the world! I want to get off!" But if you are a believer, you can stand secure in God's Word to you. Believers just aren't the kind of people that shout and holler at God. Some of the most powerful times you will ever have with God are the times you spend in silence. When you are hurting so bad that you can't say a word, when all you have the strength to do is groan and nobody but God knows what you're going through, God's presence will see you through! We don't have to bow our heads in defeat and in despair. The way to get through a zero hour is to simply decide to face reality with faith.

---

*Christianity doesn't make life easier,
but it does give us the strength to face life.*

It is time for Christians to understand that the purpose of Christianity is not to avoid difficulty. It is to nurture the strength of God's character resident in us to offset any difficulty when it comes. Before the devil got to Job, he had to ask God for permission. And before the devil can get to you with that problem or that situation, he has to obtain God's permission. Half the trouble that you're going through has come because you're just simply being set up for a miracle!

There hath no temptation taken you but such as is common to man: but God is faithful, who will not suffer you to be tempted above that ye are able; but will with the temptation also make a way to escape, that ye may be able to bear it (1 Corinthians 10:13).

When it looks like all hell has broken loose in my life, I have a supreme confidence that God will not allow anything to knock me out of the race because His Word declares it! He may allow me to face a problem that illuminates my utter weakness and drives me even closer to the strength of God. He may allow me to enter the flames so He can show His delivering power in the midst of those flames, and I can come out of that test and trial stronger than ever before. I've come to finally understand that many times, I'm going through a trial for someone else, not just for me.

Christianity doesn't make life easier, but it does give us the strength to face life. Christianity doesn't remove the red lights, the stumps, or even the tragedies from life. However, our walk with Christ gives us divine vitality, supernatural armor, and the tough skin and battle smarts we need to deliver others in Jesus' name! Mature Christians are marked by cool-headedness in battle. They demonstrate a proven stability to stand calm and collected in Christ, even in the midst of a storm!

Chapter 9

Fight Fire With Fire!

The devil had done his best to kill me before I ever reached womanhood. Then after I met and married Wayne, we had survived two unexpected pregnancies while we were still in college. Our first daughter was born, and my life was saved when an angel assisted with the birth in answer to the prayers of a man of God. Only ten months after the birth of our second daughter, I was diagnosed with advanced cancer of the cervix. Again satan wanted to strike me down, but God intervened supernaturally.

We survived total financial failure and answered the call of God to preach the gospel to the people of inner city Inglewood, California, then the enemy suddenly turned his focus on my husband. First came the near-fatal heart attack in Hawaii, while our daughters were still young. We were beginning to climb above many of our financial and physical struggles of the early years when Wayne was suddenly attacked and viciously beaten in a car theft gone awry.

For days, Wayne hovered between life and death as belivers joined in prayer on his behalf across the world, while the news media played devil's advocate with speculation and rumors on the prime-time news. In the end, God raised Wayne from his bed in spite of the gloomy predictions of the neurologists who were trying to stop his brain hemorrhage.

My "small moment" of pain was almost over when I saw preachers who I knew couldn't stand each other gather together outside the Intensive Care Unit just before they went in to pray for my dying husband. They had to repent before the Lord and hug one another before they could pray together for another.

I knew the "moment" was almost over when at least 19 members of my husband's family walked into the church after God miraculously healed him from this assault. I saw my sister-in-law in particular, who had abandoned God years ago, begin to go over the miracles and the miraculous things that God had done. I watched her lift her hand and say, "God is good" just before she began to speak in other tongues with an explosion of joy! I knew my "moment" was almost over when backsliders called the house around the clock to say, "Tell Pastor Davis that I remember every message, and I'm coming back to God."

After miraculously surviving all those challenges and more, we next faced the crisis of a severe viral attack on Wayne's lungs while he was ministering to believers in Haiti. This was followed by a bout of tuberculosis.

What could happen next? We found that out several years later when Wayne was diagnosed as having an inoperable brain tumor. The doctors predicted, at most, he would survive 6-12 months with radiation and less than

90 days without it. Once again, we had come face-to-face with a zero hour. I will never forget those grueling days when Wayne was so sick that he couldn't return to his duties as bishop and pastor. I had to keep preaching, teaching, and administrating despite the pain and anguish I was feeling inside.

Finally, I came to the point one day when I became so tired that I screamed, "Lord, I am *not* doing another women's conference! I won't do another revival or leadership meeting either, not until You heal Wayne! Do you hear me, Lord?!"

I'm sure you see the humor in this. There I was, an angry 135-pound woman shaking my fist at my Creator and threating to go "on strike" if I didn't get my miracle! If this mighty God, my Creator, had simply thought the desire to see me "removed" from His sight, I would have been less than a memory in the blink of an eye! Yet God, in His grace, mercy, and gentle understanding, simply smiled and said:

I don't have to heal Wayne in the way you think I should. I will do what brings Me glory and honor. You want to pray for Wayne and go all over the country saying, "I prayed and God delivered." Well, this time it won't work. Seek Me for My will. Set your heart to labor and obey Me—regardless of what I do for you. Obey Me because of who I am to you. I am your God, and I am the God of all flesh. I am the God of the living and the dead. Recognize My power, respect My authority, and praise My glory.

I repented and wiped my eyes. And, at the very next opportunity, I began to preach again. I began to realize that I served the same Jesus who entered a place where hundreds of desperately ill people were waiting and searching for a miracle. Yet He only healed *one man*, and then He continued on His journey. He healed only one man, not because He didn't love the others too, but because His Father had only instructed Him to heal the one man and then go.

---

*Miracles take place
because of the will and timing
of the Father, not simply in response
to the immediate needs of the people.*

Two years later, I was grieving in a room of the funeral home where my late husband's body lay in state. Suddenly, Rev. E.V. Hill walked briskly into the room and said, "The Lord talked to me today about you, and He told me to give you this message: 'What does it mean for a man to receive healing? It means he is *free from pain and sickness*. Yes, the enemy wants you to believe that your husband was *not healed*. But is it not true that this day he is free from pain and sickness?' "

As I nodded my head in agreement, a smile came over my face as I realized that *even in death, God heals!* Sometimes, death is the vehicle that sets us free! I had experienced being "forsaken for a small moment" once again, and again, I felt that moment fully pass.

You may be suffering right now "for a small moment." Learn to praise God in the midst of your pain. Grow up in Him and become a living sacrifice, for your moment is almost up!

I have asked God, "Lord, many times You ask me to do things that are too difficult for me to do. Couldn't You just 'speak the word' and leave me out of the miracle?" What I have begun to learn is that we often ask God to undo what *we* have done! God's answer is simple: "I want you to do what you *can* do so that I will have space to do what you *can't* do in your life."

Have you ever been with someone who caught a glimpse of God in their hospital room or on their deathbed? In every case, their faith is stirred up and renewed. They get a new desire to live and to trust God to heal them—until all the moaning saints drag into their room.

There always seems to be one sour apple in the barrel that just has to say something like, "Child, I hate to see you like this. Why I had a cousin who had the same thing...but she didn't make it." That poor saint they are visiting is battling death and telling himself, "I know He is able" while his "uplifting visitor" is dumping doubt, unbelief, and endless tales of dying into the room. (Visiting the sick is a ministry of *faith*. If you don't have it, then *stay home*! Keep your unbelief and doubt out of the hearing of those who are believing God for a miracle—or their sickness could be on your head!)

Too many of us fret and panic when the going gets tough. I know we have to be "real" and transparent with God, but there is some truth in what Robert Schuller says: "When the going gets tough, the tough get going!" The tough just don't just die and fall off; they just say, "Well, it looks like we have another situation for You and me to work out, Lord! I'm not moving anywhere until I hear from You. But when you speak and show me what to do, I'm moving out!"

Too many of us move out before we even know what to do! The only remedy for the zero hour crisis in our lives is found in the Word of God. If you want to be standing when the flames die down, then you need to get into God's Word and start believing. Your zero hour crisis should not find you unprepared, but it will if you don't find your source of power and learn how to tap it.

There is no substitute for knowing the power of God's Word. You have to learn about and walk in the power that is in His name—Jesus Christ. You have to know what His blood did for you at Calvary. Every passing minute is a matter of life and death for someone torn by the conflicts of a difficult problem. Satan keeps knocking at every door. Not one of us are exempt. He'll break windows and try every door in his efforts to get into your life, because he despises you and the power you have in Jesus' name. He is totally devoted to his mission to kill, steal, and destroy.

Can you withstand the onslaught of satan? Think about this situation: If you were to get word right now that your mamma and daddy had died along with your kids, could you handle it? If you learned that your spouse had just been murdered by thugs, could you handle it? What if your house was destroyed by fire on the same afternoon that you lost your job? Would you be able to handle it?

Do you realize that *every problem* you could ever face *already contains the seed of God's solution?* Everything the devil brings against you in your life contains its solution if you would really examine it.

There is no substitute for knowing the power of God's Word.

God declared through the prophet Isaiah, "No weapon that is formed against thee shall prosper" (Is. 54:17a). Who in their right mind would have the nerve to mess with someone who was impervious to every weapon you could ever bring against them? Don't get shook up by the enemy's latest scheme to bring you down—God wasn't caught by surprised, so why should you be worried? He has already guaranteed that scheme, weapon, or attack is not going to prosper!

Let the lady talk about you at work, and let the neighbors start fussing about your kids (as long as you know your kids are in line). Let your husband act like a fool; let your wife "go crazy" on you. Love them and declare the truth: "Don't you know what God said? No weapon, no weapon, no weapon, no weapon that is formed against you is going to prosper?"

The devil can set up his artillery, but it won't work. He can try depression, but that won't work either. He has already tried anger, and that didn't work. He's already worn himself out with the poverty thing, and that didn't work either once the Word of God took root. In desperation that defeated foe just might say, "All right. I'll walk death into your life! (Nothing else seems to work!)" Just remind him what happened with the Lord Jesus Christ, the apostle Peter, and the apostle Paul, just to name just a few. He "walked death" into their lives, and their preaching and teaching ministries instantly jumped across time into every generation since Christ! Just keep on praising God!

One of the most effective ways to battle a forest fire is to start a back fire, a controlled fire that removes every stick of fuel from the path of the out-of-control blaze. Have you ever noticed that whenever a bacterial infection or a virus invades your body you get a fever? Doctors say that is the body's natural defense against these organisms. The human body is much tougher than most of these invading diseases, so a high temperature will kill far more attacking cells than those native to our bodies.

> *Understand therefore this day, that the Lord thy God is He which goeth over before thee; **as a consuming fire He** shall destroy them, and He shall bring them down before thy face: so shalt thou drive them out, and destroy them quickly, as the Lord hath said unto thee* (Deuteronomy 9:3).

Hebrews 12:29 echoes this Old Testament passage as it says, "For our God is a consuming fire." He is a jealous God who doesn't appreciate anyone or anything messing with His chosen people. He doesn't appreciate anyone lying about Him or His Word, and He takes any attack or insult against *you* as a personal attack and insult against *Him*! If you lean totally on Him, you have just "linked arms" and joined forces with the Consuming Fire who made you.

Scripture also says God "...maketh His angels spirits, and His ministers a *flame of fire*" (Heb. 1:7). The Holy Spirit is directly associated with fire. John the Baptist told his disciples that Jesus Christ would baptize believers "with the Holy Ghost *and with fire*" (Mt. 3:11; Lk. 3:16)! The best way to fight the fires of adversity is with the *fire of God!*

All strength and power emanates from *one* source in the universe and beyond—God Almighty. Scripture says your strength is in the joy of the Lord (Neh. 8:10). You already know the devil's attacks aren't going to prosper against you. They may knock you down, but they won't take you out of the race—you have God's Word on it! No one, and no thing or force, can take away your joy in the Lord. Why? Because your *joy is not built on happiness!* Your joy is founded upon the Chief Cornerstone, who cannot and will not be moved.

When you get tired, weak, worn, or depressed (yes, Christians *do* get this way sometimes if they're doing anything at all to rile the devil); if you feel sad and uptight; you need to run to the secret place: Get into God and His Word! I've discovered that no matter what I face, when I get into God's Word, I get into His strength! When I get into His strength, I also get into His joy! Everytime I get close to my Father God, I'm cuddling up with a Consuming Fire! I start getting hot about the things of God! I start declaring God's Word with new authority and power! I start revealing and manifesting the God that lives within me! I find that I step back and God steps up to bat! *It is time to fight fire with the Fire!*

God said, "Call unto Me, and I will answer thee, and shew thee great and mighty things, which thou knowest not" (Jer. 33:3). You may be facing a situation in which you don't know what to do—*I dare you to get off that phone and get on your knees!* Quit running to your relatives and telling your mamma all your problems "so she'll pray for you." (Don't get me wrong, praying mamma's are one of God's greatest resources, but He really wants *you* to do some praying!)

Quit crying to the doctor down the street—he's running out of medications for all your "indications." Quit gossiping, I mean, "talking" to the deacon and the preacher about all the "sin" you see in the people and in your enemies; it is time to call upon the name of the Lord!

God is the source of all strength and power.

God will show you everything you need to know. That little mamma in the church may not have the answer for you this time, but Jesus says, "I made you. You're mine. I know what's going on with you. If you want to know how to get it fixed, ask Me!"

Too many of us are too busy nursing and nourishing our pride over "being perfect." Pardon my English, but "You ain't!" I challenge you right now to say, "God, please fix it. You know my problem. I need an answer." There is an answer for *every problem* in the Word of God!

Paul said, "For if, when we were enemies, we were reconciled to God by the death of His Son, much more, being reconciled, we shall be saved *by His life*" (Rom. 5:10). Don't you know that you are saved by His life? I don't care who your psychotherapist is! I'm not impressed that you pay $150 an hour! What do you get for your money? If he's not talking the life of Jesus, then he doesn't have the answer for your life! He's got problems too.

I heard someone call Jesus a Wonder-working Wonder. I like to think He is the Powerful Power, the Marvelous Marvel, the Joyous Joy, and the Magnificently

Magnificent! There is nothing going on in my life that is too big for Jesus to handle! I don't care what it is—He can handle it all. Sometimes when you're going through the valley, or feeling faint from the fire, it is easy to feel like everybody has forgotten you. You've done what you know to do, but you still have your problem and the answer hasn't come forth yet. What do you do? Remember God's Word, and don't stop short of victory!

God hasn't forgotten you.

For a small moment have I forsaken thee... (Isaiah 54:7).

That rugged week and that mind-boggling month through which you've been waiting for God to resolve the problems of your zero hour is nothing but a *small moment*. I know the devil is taunting you almost minute-by-minute, whispering, "Where is your God now? Look at what is going on in your life! You've been jumping and shouting and talking about how the Lord will 'make a way' somehow. Well...where is He *now?*"

God hasn't forgotten you! I like to think that in that small moment He is at work somewhere fixing things. Have you ever stepped into a prayer line and asked the brother or sister who is ministering to you, "Pray for me that I get a raise," or, "Pray for me that I get a promotion." Think about what is involved in answering that prayer. For you to become manager, the manager has to become a vice president! That means the vice president has to become the president. If all that is to take place, the *current* president has to die or the other manager's wife has to get a promotion back East so he can move!

Sometimes, God "moves mountains" and "changes the hearts of kings" to answer prayers offered in line with His will and purposes, but in every case, He only answers prayer His way, according to His divine timetable. The problem is that some (if not most of us impatient Americans) want it all *now*! "Well Lord, I got in the line today! So when I go to work tomorrow, I want it." It takes a *small moment* for God to perfect His work in you—He has a greater agenda than you and I. He is also out to "…let patience have her perfect work" in us (Jas. 1:4a)!

If somebody told you, "Just ask Him today and He'll do it today because He's a *right-now* God!" then somebody lied to you! My Bible says, "One day is with the Lord as a thousand years" (2 Pet. 3:8). God may not be bound by time like we are, but there is one all-important fact that you cannot afford to forget:

> *Just because God doesn't come through today doesn't mean that He's not on the way!*

When the devil tells you that God has forsaken you; when he tries to shake your faith by asking, "Where is your God now?" answer him with the rock-solid Word of God! That is the foundation of your power! God committed His promises to you in a contract form that will never fade away. It is a "sure prophecy" and revelation of God's good intentions for you! Don't try to impress the deceiver with stale boasts from years and days gone by. Don't try to drive him away by saying, "Look devil, I want to inform you and your legions that I may be broke this year, *but in 1976 I wasn't broke!*"

I'm telling you, he won't be impressed. But do you know what will impress and depress him? He hates it when he runs into a saint who is neck-deep in troubles, but who nevertheless slaps him in the face with Psalm 34:6: "This poor man cried, and the Lord heard him, and saved him out of all his troubles." You ought to tell the devil, "If you keep whispering in my ear, I'm going to start crying out to God, and you know what happens then, don't you devil? When I cry out in Jesus' name, then my Lord is going to hear me. And He is not going to be happy about your lies and whispers. The more you hassle me, the more I'll pray. The more you trouble and afflict me, the more I'll fast and pray and praise the name of Jesus, the King of kings and Lord of lords! You might as well give up now, satan, because as always, the Lord is going to save me!"

Don't let the devil mess with your faith.

You've got to play rough with the devil. He likes to fight dirty and illegally because he has no legal right to you anymore. He knows some of the things that he had you do before you were saved, and he even knows what you've pulled since you got saved. He will take it upon himself to be your self-appointed "memory." That is why he is called the "accuser of the brethren" (Rev. 12:10). He may have you feeling low and guilty right now. You may be hoping that nobody opens up that closet hiding your secret sins and failures.

When you get tired and feel all burned out, when you feel like you don't want to go any further, go to God's Word. When you find yourself saying, "I just want to get out of the choir," or "I'm not going to usher or teach anymore," and especially when you are to the point where you say, "I don't even want to come to church and be taught anymore," quote Isaiah 40:31: "But they that wait upon the Lord shall renew their strength; they shall mount up with wings as eagles; they shall run, and not be weary; and they shall walk, and not faint."

The deceiver wants you to think you are a "turkey saint," but God says you are like an eagle! You have power and authority. You are going to run and not be weary; you will walk and not faint! The devil will take his bag of lies and retreat from you when you strike him with the Sword of Truth!

Don't you let the devil mess with your faith. If you are rooted in God's unchanging Word and led daily by His abiding Spirit, then you are a child of God! You will not be moved by what you see! You will not be moved by what you hear! You won't even be moved by what other people think! The only thing that will move you is the truth—the things you know are truth by God's Word.

If God *says* He is a healer, then that is exactly what He means! It is time for every blood-washed believer to stand on God's Word and start telling the devil he is a liar! Any time the devil is bold enough to get in your ear and whisper his lies, you ought to be bold enough to shout the Word of God back to him! (He probably won't enjoy your company much.)

I can see them beating Jesus. I can see Him hanging on the cross. I saw the blood and water come out of His side, and I heard the Word say, "By His stripes ye were healed," (1 Pet. 2:24). When I saw them beat Him, in my mind's eye I saw pneumonia hanging on that tree. When they hit Him the second time, I saw tuberculosis in the lungs. When they got up there to hit him again, I saw arthritis, I saw hypertension, I saw ulcers in the stomach, and I saw cancer. All of that was on the cross, for Jesus was hung up for your hang-ups. You don't have to be bothered by the devil and his mess.

When you are face-to-face with a zero hour, when it looks like all hell is breaking loose and nothing is turning out right, just tell that devil, "In Jesus' name, get back!" Pick up your ammunition. I know that somewhere in the 66 anointed books of the Sword of the Spirit, the living Word of God, there is a word for you! Get ready to bruise satan's head with the Seed of Heaven! Fight fire with fire!

You may find yourself in the lion's den like Daniel, or in a fiery furnace like the three Hebrew boys. Whatever your zero hour brings, if you go in with Jesus, you will come back out with Jesus. He will never desert you. Remember, He loved you and died for you *even though He knew what you are like*! He won't leave you just because your head "isn't right" yet. God doesn't leave you just because your body becomes sick, muttering, "Yep, he sinned." God doesn't leave you just because you lose all your money and you can't "give in the offering" like you used to. God, the Son, promised, "Lo, I am with you alway, even unto the end of the world" (Mt. 28:20). He will never leave you nor forsake you (see Heb. 13:5). He knows what you're going through, and He will give you power in your zero hour!

God knows every thought and fear that is running through your mind and emotions right now. He knows if you have dropped out of college or suddenly quit your job. He knows if you have left your husband or wife—He also knows why and who was involved. Perhaps you just dropped out of life after everything around you seemed to "push you out."

God knows what you are going through, and His anointing will destroy every yoke in your life!

Perhaps your husband, your wife, or your children have you stuck in some corner through their words and actions. God is going to build you up—right now, right where you are at. It is no accident that you picked up this book—He wanted to meet you here. Perhaps you've heard other ministers say, "You don't have a ministry, so sit down and shut up!" God says, "I am going to cause you to bring deliverance to those who rejected you. The relatives who laughed at you and mocked you will come for you to feed them the Bread of Life!"

Acts 1:8a says, "But ye shall receive power, after that the Holy Ghost is come upon you." Look at all the non-believers you know and work with. When they hit rock bottom, God says *you* are the one who will lift them up in His name! Yes, I'm talking about you, the "Holy Roller," the tongue-talking one: God is going to make you a name and a praise among all the people. He is about to turn back your captivity right before your eyes! The devil thought he had you all wrapped up and tied up. He has done his best to utterly destroy you—he tried it on Jesus too! God will glorify Himself through you by taking you from "nothing" to *something*! Then He is going to let you watch as He sovereignly takes hold of your finances and transforms them from ashes to gold!

He is going to let you see Him take you from death's door and raise you up with His power. He is going to let you see Him do it because He is the Lord thy God, and if He tells you that He's going to let you see Him do it, then He's going to let you see Him do it! Don't waste time wondering "How?"; that's none of your business! Just wipe your eyes and get ready to watch Him in action!

His anointing shall destroy every yoke in your life! No, it won't be the songs that do it—it will be the *Holy Ghost* on the songs! It won't be the preachers that do it, it will be the Holy Ghost on them. When the Holy Ghost falls on you, everything else falls off of you! The fire within you is about to burn out and extinguish the fires around you!

You may find yourself crying, but I hear the Word of God say, "Weeping may endure for a night, but joy cometh in the morning" (Ps. 30:5b). You may have to go to bed with your handkerchief or tissue, but don't forget your dancing shoes! Put them right by the side of your bed! No matter how long the night may seem, when the light of morning comes—and it *will*—rise with the Son and put on your dancing shoes, for the delivering arm of your Lord has come!

Epilogue

"Oh God, my God, my wonderful Savior, please help me, help me! The hospital has just called and told me to return as soon as possible. It seems I just left only a moment ago. Wayne is there suffering... Lord, I have never seen him in so much pain. But even in his pain he's not complaining or doubting You. He's lying there, those big eyes pleading for relief from the pain. Lord, how much more can he take? Lord, how much more can all of us—his family, his church, his friends—take? Please, Lord, come by today and help us; the fires and flames of trial and tribulation are intensifying.

"Whitney and Timothy have just gotten married. I watched my baby daughter weep, in the midst of her joy, because her dad was not there to perform the ceremony. Lord, what can we do? Thank You for our wonderful family physician who recommended that the entire wedding party come to the hospital and let Wayne see his baby all dressed in white.

"Well, Lord...we got through that. Oh yes, in the midst of the furnace, thanks so much, Lord, for all the beautiful friends in the gospel who blessed us financially so that Whitney could have the wedding of her dreams. You know them name by name, family by family. When the enemy laughed and said, 'Cancel the wedding,' Lord, You gave us the last laugh when the phone rang and Dr. Ernestine Reems spoke prophetically that we were to cancel nothing, that You would provide and that we would not owe a dime when the wedding was over! Lord, we did get the last laugh because You performed Your word just like You said You would.

"Oh God, then there were our birthdays—my birthday on April 3, Wayne's fiftieth birthday on April 9, and Wendy, our oldest daughter, who turned 23 on April 5. Tucked between those birthdays was my twenty-fourth wedding anniversary on the fifth of April. Lord, when I thought my heart would break in half, you allowed a special sister in Christ to stop by and take me to dinner to celebrate in spite of my fiery trials. What fun it was to indulge ourselves at the Benihana Japanese Restaurant. But now, Lord, it's April 16, and the driver is rushing my dad and I to the hospital. In my heart I know it's for the last time. I can't take it Lord.... Please, couldn't You give us one more miracle. Couldn't You just touch Wayne's body and heal him. Couldn't You just make him whole. Couldn't You just take his pain and sickness away. I know You can; I believe You and Your Word."

When we were about ten minutes away from the hospital I literally began to have difficulty breathing. My lungs seemed to about to burst with the pain. I slumped over in my seat and tried desperately tried to open the back window in an attempt to get more air into the car. When my father reached over to hold me the Holy Spirit whispered, "You know what is happening." In my mind and in my heart I began to scream, *No, no, no! Please God, Don't let Wayne die. Help him to hold on.* As we raced into the Intensive Care Unit, several doctors and nurses were standing by and moved to the side. My precious dad and I began praying and singing, "Peace, peace, what a wonderful peace...coming down from the heavens above, sweep over my spirit forever I pray...."

"As we sang and prayed, God, Your peace that surpasses all understanding slipped into that hospital room and You caught Wayne up in Your arms and very gently took his last breath. Your presence in that room was so quiet and sweet that I didn't realize Wayne had slipped away until one of his precious physicians said, 'God has him on the other side now.' "

Over the next few days it seemed as though a great fog, a mist, had rolled over my mind, spirit, emotions, and even my body. I simply had to put one foot in front of the other. When the enemy would haunt me and whisper, 'Where is your God? Where is God's manifested healing?' all I could hang onto were the powerful words of Rev. E.V. Hill, whom God sent to minister to me. Rev. Hill told me that he knew the enemy had tried to make me doubt that God was a healer because Wayne had gone home to be with the Lord. Then he gave me a definition of healing that I will never forget. He stated, "What is healing? Healing is when one is free from pain and sickness." He reminded me that Bishop Wayne Davis was free from pain and sickness. Again, I was able to laugh and rejoice in spite of the attack of the enemy.

Two weeks after Wayne's death I was invited to my best friend's bridal shower. I was hurting so bad that I did not wish to attend. However, a precious brother and sister in the Lord encouraged me to go...and even made it possible. It was the first time I had gone out socially in a long time. Although I have a public ministry, I really am very private as a person. I recall that it was difficult to walk into that bridal shower knowing that there would be so many people there. I wanted to go into a corner and hide, but everywhere I went the Lord sent someone to love and comfort me. Before the night was over, six different beautiful women of God came and prophesied at different times the same message, "What we do tonight for our sister we shall do for you soon." Each was sensitive to the fact that I had recently lost my husband.

By the time the shower was over I was overwhelmed that God would give me that much attention even at a social gathering. I went home with grief in one hand but hope in the other. I went home crying, but before the night was over I was laughing at what I term "the audacity of God." God slips in when you least expect it to encourage, lift up, and heal. While I was yet crying, He brought me joy that allowed me to laugh. Exactly 12 months from the night of that bridal shower, I fulfilled God's prophecy for my life and married a wonderful, kind, gentle, and loving man, Andrew C. Turner II. Just like God promised, I went from grieving to grinning! Even in death, God allowed me to laugh.

Additional copies of this book and other
book titles from DESTINY IMAGE are
available at your local bookstore.

For a complete list of our titles,
visit us at www.destinyimage.com
Send a request for a catalog to:

Destiny Image® Publishers, Inc.
P.O. Box 310
Shippensburg, PA 17257-0310

*"Speaking to the Purposes of God for This
Generation and for the Generations to Come"*